Seashells of North Carolina

Hugh J. Porter & Lynn Houser
Photographs by Scott D. Taylor • Edited by Jeannie Faris Norris

North Carolina Sea Grant College Program
UNC-SG-97-03

North Carolina Sea Grant College Program
Box 8605, North Carolina State University
Raleigh, NC 27695-8605
919/515-2454
1997
UNC-SG-97-03

NC seagrant.org

This book is based on *Sea Shells Common to North Carolina*, written by Hugh J. Porter and Jim Tyler and published in 1971 by the North Carolina Sea Grant College Program. A revised edition was published in 1981.

In 1994, North Carolina Sea Grant agreed to fund a complete revision, which has evolved into a publication with a new title, updated common and scientific names, revised species descriptions and text, new photographs and 82 additional species. The book was expanded to cover common mollusks that are small and mollusks that are collected by scuba divers in North Carolina's outer waters.

Members of the North Carolina shell club and scuba divers such as Mark Johnson of Wilmington provided comments helpful in the preparation of this book. Lawrence Eaton of the N.C. Division of Environmental Management made suggestions about mollusks common in northern estuarine waters of North Carolina.

The mollusk collection at the University of North Carolina Institute of Marine Sciences was a significant source of data and specimens used for photos. Much of this collection was secured from commercial fishing catches and from research vessels belonging to the UNC Institute of Marine Sciences, N.C. Department of Environment and Natural Resources and Duke University Marine Laboratory. Additional specimens were photographed from the personal collections of Johnson and Porter.

This work was supported by Grant NA46RGO087 from the National Sea Grant College Program, National Oceanic and Atmospheric Administration, to the North Carolina Sea Grant College Program and by the UNC Institute of Marine Sciences.

Introduction

For many people, seashells are just part of the beach scenery — thousands of pretty but nameless objects strewn along the shore. Other people know the names of shells but often wonder how they were formed and what type of animal lived inside. Such incidental knowledge may not seem important, but it can encourage people to observe their environment more closely and to gain a better understanding of it. As a result, they may become better fishers, more informed teachers or more conscientious stewards of our coast. To this end, the seashell guide was produced.

Many collectors get started when they find an intriguing shell, perhaps after a storm, and search for it in a guide. Others, by chance, meet an experienced sheller on the beach. Talking with a collector passionate about shells is likely to spark an interest in anyone who has spent time at the coast.

A walk down the beach is never the same once you begin to recognize a few shells. Gradually, you learn to use certain marks to solve the puzzle of shell identification. The walk becomes more satisfying as you recognize familiar shells like old friends, and it becomes more exciting as you look for new ones.

Experienced shell collectors know a piece of wet driftwood may be full of wood-boring clams. Shellers carefully search sea fans for tiny simnias. They scan fields of marsh grass for periwinkles. With practice, their sharpened eyes spot clam holes in the mud and identify tracks left by moonsnails. They recognize some new shells from pictures they have seen. Others send them scurrying for their guides.

The tides continually wash ashore and expose shells, some beautifully sculptured or colorful and others just unusual. It's as if the sea provides beachgoers with a natural treasure hunt. At any time, a group of shells lying inconspicuously in the sand may contain a rarity, just waiting to catch someone's eye.

Collectors learn more than just the names of shells. They become familiar with the animals that live inside and when and where certain shells are likely to be found. Shell collectors learn about tides and the physical features of the coast. They discover that many shell identification marks relate to the animal's anatomy and provide clues to its lifestyle and behavior. Before long, collectors have learned biology, physics and geography without even realizing it.

The animal that lives inside a shell is called a mollusk. More than 1,000 kinds of mollusks reportedly live in North Carolina's estuaries and ocean. Many shells are small and rare, found only in deep offshore waters. The 179 species included in the original version of this book were limited to shells of unusual interest and to common species large enough to be spotted easily by collectors. To this revision, 82 species have been added. Some were observed or collected by scuba divers, while others were small shells often found in oceanfront beach drift. In January 1995, author Hugh Porter scraped up a bucketful of shell hash from a low tide area of Bogue Banks. It contained whole shells and pieces representing 109 species.

• Mollusks

General features: Mollusk means soft-bodied. A mollusk has no skeleton — rather, its shell acts as an external skeleton. Mollusks usually have some version of a head, soft body and foot, but these features vary among groups. Bivalves, such as oysters and clams, have a mouth but no head. Clams have a strong foot for digging; oysters, however, don't need one because they attach to a surface and remain there permanently.

One important part of a mollusk's body is the mantle, the fleshy tissue that lines the inside of the shell. It is responsible for shell growth and color, and it assists in other functions such as respiration.

Most shells have a brownish "outer skin" called a periostracum while they are alive. Interestingly, the shell's beautiful colors and patterns are hidden by this covering during life. Only after the animal dies and the periostracum is lost is the shell's surface revealed.

A prime characteristic of the mollusca is its variability. Collectors must be aware of the variations possible in the shell and soft parts used to identify mollusk species.

Bivalves

Bivalves are mollusks with two shells, called valves, hinged together. One or more strong muscles inside the shell keep it closed, and a rubbery ligament near the hinge holds the shell open.

Respiration: A bivalve breathes by circulating water within its shell. The incoming water brings oxygen, and the outgoing water takes away carbon dioxide and other wastes. In some bivalves, the mantle extends into the water as a pair of tubes, called siphons. Water enters one siphon, and wastes leave through the other. In bivalves without siphons, water is exchanged through openings in the mantle.

Feeding: Bivalves generally depend on water circulation for food. Incoming water contains tiny particles of plants and animals. The gills collect this matter and move it toward the mouth. Some bivalves — oysters, scallops, mussels, venus clams and cockles — are suspension feeders. Their siphons draw in particles suspended in the water. Other bivalves — such as tellin clams, macomas and abras — are deposit feeders. Their siphons act as vacuum cleaners, sucking in the surrounding particle-filled mud. Because these animals can ingest contaminants along with the water and mud they take in, it is important to keep rivers and coastal waters clean.

Locomotion: Some bivalves have a strong foot that they expand and contract to pull themselves along the bottom or to burrow into sand or mud. Others spin a strong thread, called a byssus, that they use to anchor to rocks and other objects. Some scallops and limas "swim" by clapping their two valves together and ejecting water from the back of their shells.

Reproduction: Most bivalves have separate sexes, but some are hermaphrodites, which means they are both male and female. Depending on the species, hermaphrodites may have male and female organs or they may switch sexes at different stages of their lives. Species with simultaneous male and female organs usually release eggs and sperm at different times so they do not fertilize themselves. This allows for more genetic variation in the young.

Most bivalves release eggs and sperm directly into the water, where fertilization takes place. The fertilized eggs hatch into young called larvae that swim with other microscopic animals in the plankton. The animal matures within several weeks and settles on the bottom to develop into an adult.

The amount of time the young spend swimming differs by species, but the longer they swim, the greater the chances the currents will carry them to new environments. Many young are "wasted" because they arrive at a location where they can't survive. But this dispersal strategy has advantages because it allows populations to colonize suitable new habitats. These new populations are especially important if disaster eliminates the species from its parent habitat.

Identification aids: Both the outside and inside of a shell provide clues for identifying the bivalve and understanding how its inhabitant lived. The number and arrangement of teeth on the hinge can be used to identify and classify a bivalve. Oval-shaped muscle scars inside the shell show where the muscles attached. When two muscle scars are present, a line can connect them. This pallial line indicates where the animal's mantle, or fleshy tissue, attached to the shell. In some shells, the line curves inward, forming a pallial sinus. The size of the sinus shows how far aside the animal had to move its mantle to make room for the siphons when it closed its shell.

A large pallial sinus identifies an animal that burrowed deep into the sand or mud. To do so, it needed long siphons. Similarly, a small pallial sinus indicates that the animal had short siphons and burrowed just below the surface. A shell with no pallial sinus once housed an animal that had no siphons and lived on top of the sand or mud or attached to hard surfaces such as rocks or other shells.

Gastropods

A gastropod, or univalve, is a mollusk covered by a single coiled shell in its earliest stages and generally throughout its adult life. However, in some gastropods, the shell is present only during the larval period. The gastropod body emerges from an opening, or aperture, to eat and move.

The outside edge of the aperture is called a lip.

Each turn of a gastropod's spiral shell is a whorl. The last and usually largest whorl is the body whorl. All whorls above the body whorl make up the spire. The aperture is at the front of the shell; the spire is at the back.

Unlike bivalves, gastropods have a head with tentacles. The tentacles bear sense organs such as the eyes, which detect shadows and movement.

Many gastropods have a trap door, or operculum, attached to their foot. This structure seals the aperture opening when the animal retreats into its shell.

Respiration: Like bivalves, most gastropods breathe by taking in oxygen from the water. They may have one or two siphons.

Feeding: Gastropods have more structures for feeding than bivalves, so they don't depend on water circulation for food. Most gastropods are carnivores that feed on other animals. A few primitive gastropods are herbivores, or plant-eaters. A few are omnivores, which eat both plants and animals. Others are scavengers or detritivores, which eat dead plant and animal matter. A gastropod's head has a tubelike extension called a proboscis with a mouth and a ribbonlike strip of teeth called a radula. Both are used for feeding. Herbivores use the radula to scrape algae off rocks, while carnivores use it to tear flesh or to drill holes in shells.

In most of the cones, terebras and turrids, the radular teeth are poisonous stingers or darts capable of narcotizing or killing their prey. Some cones have poison-carrying darts that they toss at their prey. No cones in North Carolina waters are documented as poisonous to humans, but a few Pacific cones are capable of killing people.

Because they vary little within a species, radula are important indicators of gastropod identity and relationship to other species.

Locomotion: Most gastropods move along the bottom by sending a series of ripples through their muscular foot. Janthinas, however, spend their lives floating in the open ocean attached to "rafts" of bubbles.

Reproduction: Fertilization of gastropod eggs occurs both inside and outside the body. The eggs are frequently laid in gelatinlike blobs or in one of many types of egg capsules. Egg capsules are often seen washed up on the beach and mistaken for seaweed. In some species, the eggs hatch into swimming forms. In others, they hatch into crawling forms that resemble adults. Some females bear live young.

• Shell Growth

A mollusk produces its shell from glands in the edge of the mantle. The basic component of a shell is calcium carbonate. Another ingredient is a protein substance called conchiolin. The mantle uses minerals from seawater and its food to form a matrix, or latticework, of conchiolin. The shell grows as calcium carbonate crystals form on the conchiolin lattice or on other calcium crystals.

The smoothness of the shell depends on the smoothness of the mantle. Shells with large spines or ridges are formed in species with ruffly mantles. As the animal grows, the mantle and the shell grow too.

Most mollusks attain their mature size in one to six years. The **bay scallop** reaches its maximum size in two years and rarely survives a third season. Some periwinkles have been kept in captivity for more than 10 years. Yet growth ring counts of a **southern quahog** from offshore Shackleford Banks suggest it lived 77 years or more.

• Shell Color

Both the shell and the mantle contain color pigments. Pigments from food eaten by the mollusk concentrate in color cells along the mantle's edge. These cells produce patterns on the shell such as dots, circles and stripes. Bands of color occur when a group of cells stays in one place and produces pigment. Spots or patches result when groups of these color cells turn off and on. Zigzags occur when the cells move up and down the mantle's edge. The shell color may change slightly if a mollusk changes diet or location.

Iridescent interiors are caused not by color pigments but by the way light enters and reflects from layers of the shell's structure.

• Mollusk Habitats

Mollusks live in a variety of habitats. This guide covers mollusks that live in salt and brackish waters, but many also live in fresh water and on land.

Marine and estuarine mollusks have also adapted to many different habitats: sandy beaches, intertidal sand and mud flats, rocky bottoms, eelgrass flats and shallow to deeper-water habitats.

• Studying and Collecting Shells

Although few mollusks live on sandy beaches, the shoreline is a good place to search for empty shells that have washed ashore. The best time to look is early spring after winter storms and in September when hurricanes are active. The best time of day is an hour before or after low tide, especially during spring tides that occur on new and full moons. Walk the beaches frequently. It's good for your health, and the shells can change with every turn of the tide. Collecting can also be done on the intertidal flats of the state's many bays and estuaries. Scuba-assisted collections from offshore rocks and shipwrecks have produced species rarely found on beaches.

With permission, search the decks of offshore fishing boats and the shucking piles of seafood dealers who handle fish, shrimp or offshore scallop catches. A.F. Chestnut, an early director of the University of North Carolina Institute of Marine Sciences, found the first known living specimen of the rare **Coronado bonnet** on the deck of a trawler that had been fishing off Wimble Shoals near Oregon Inlet. Excellent mollusk specimens are sometimes found in piles at commercial scallop shucking plants in Carteret County. However, be aware that many of these shells may have been harvested from waters off New Jersey, Virginia, South Carolina, Georgia, Florida or the Gulf of Mexico. Also, protect yourself from cuts or bruises because the decaying flesh remaining on these shells could be covered with bacteria and viruses.

Don't take live specimens unless you plan to document your collection carefully enough that a scientist could use it. Only after you have collected beach shells for a while and have a well-documented collection should you begin taking live specimens. Remember, few things smell worse than a dead mollusk left in a car or a jacket pocket. If you take a live mollusk for your collection, clean or preserve it immediately.

Always take a pen and notebook to describe the shell and where and how you collected it. This is essential for anyone starting a serious collection. The most important information to record is the date, the shell's location — such as "one mile south of Cape Hatteras" — and whether the mollusk was taken dead or alive. The shell's name can be added later. It is helpful to include other details, such as the tidal conditions, habitat, what the mollusk was doing and other animals present. It's fun to look back through the notebook and reminisce about a walk on the beach after a bad storm or a warm afternoon wading in a tidal pool. Shell clubs are also interested in compiling this information.

Instead of taking live mollusks, try observing the appearance, habitat and behavior of the animals. Naturalist Rachel Carson, author of *Silent Spring*, did this as she wrote books such as *The Edge of the Sea* and *The Sea Around Us*. She used words to collect the sea life she found in tidal pools, on rocks and in estuaries. Those interested in photography can collect the animals on film. Patient observation may reveal activities such as a whelk pounding open a bivalve or a moonsnail drilling a hole into another mollusk. People interested in learning more about the mollusca would be advised to read *Living Marine Mollusca* by C.M. Yonge and T.E. Thompson or *The Shell Makers* by G. Alan Solem.

When can mollusks be observed? Unfortunately, many of them are active at night, making observation difficult. In daylight, some mollusks can be found by shoveling mud into a kitchen colander and draining it with seawater. Others can be found under rocks, which should be returned so that the tiny plants and animals living there won't perish.

• Commercial Value of Mollusks

Several types of mollusks are harvested commercially in North Carolina, and others have commercial potential. None of the state's mollusks are known to be naturally toxic, so all can be eaten if fresh. But many are too bitter, small or uncommon for commercial harvest. For example, some arks and bittersweets are eaten in the Caribbean and Far East, but they are too bitter for most Americans to enjoy. Coquinas make a delicious broth, but they are too small to be harvested economically. Oysters and other bivalves can be toxic if they come from waters that are polluted or contaminated with toxic algae. When eating bivalves, it is wise to know where they came from and to cook them thoroughly.

Several types of oysters are found along our coast, but only the **eastern oyster** (*Crassostrea virginica*) is commercially valuable. Oysters that settle in mud die, so the state and growers dump bivalve shell into estuarine areas known for excellent oyster growth to provide larvae with a firm surface to settle, attach and grow. When the oysters settle, they are called "spat." Oysters reach an edible size in two to three years. When runoff from development causes silt to cover the oyster beds, the industry suffers because the young have trouble settling and the adults grow more slowly.

Several species of scallops are gathered commercially. These include the **Atlantic bay scallop** (*Argopecten irradians concentricus*), **Atlantic calico scallop** (*Argopecten gibbus*) and **Atlantic deep-sea scallop** (*Placopecten magellanicus*). The **Atlantic bay scallop**, which is gathered most often, lives only two or three years with an average age of about 16 months.

Many people think there is only one type of clam. This isn't true. There are many types of clams, including species that are commonly eaten and economically important. The **northern quahog** (*Mercenaria mercenaria*), also known as the **hard-shelled**, **littleneck**, **cherrystone** or **chowder clam**, is an important fishery in the state's estuaries. This clam sometimes hybridizes in the inlets with the **southern quahog** (*Mercenaria campechiensis*), which is known to live offshore near Beaufort Inlet.

One important clam is a northern species with its southern limit in our state. The **soft-shell** (*Mya arenaria*), found around and above Oregon Inlet, is the fried clam of many restaurants. It reaches an edible size of 3 to 4 inches in five years of growth, and it lives about 10 years.

Another northern species, the **blue mussel**, is raised commercially in Europe and Maine, and it is an untapped resource with aquaculture potential in North Carolina. However, adults of this species seem to survive only north of Cape Hatteras. A large number of mussels can be produced in a small area because they live in large colonies on crowded mud flats. It is estimated that a 1-acre mussel bed produces up to 10,000 pounds of meat per year, compared to a 1-acre pasture that produces only 200 pounds of beef per year.

• How to Use This Guide

To identify a shell, decide first whether it is a bivalve, gastropod, chiton, tuskshell or squid. Then look under the "Descriptive Guide to Families" on pages 113 to 118. Compare the shell to the descriptions that best match its shape. If the comments apply, turn to the pages listed. Using the photographs and descriptions, find the name of the shell.

Remember that the shells included are those most likely found in North Carolina. It is possible that you will find a shell too rare or too small to be listed. If you cannot find your shell, check one of the books noted in the bibliography.

Each entry presents information on size, description, color, habitat and notes of interest about the shell or the animal that lives inside. The size listed is the maximum collected in North Carolina (from records of the North Carolina Shell Club or the University of North Carolina Institute of Marine Sciences collection). The information on habitat describes where the animal is known to live in North Carolina; in other places, the same shell may be found at different depths. The habitat description also notes where you may find specimens washed ashore. Descriptions of the shells use everyday language except for a few terms commonly used to describe parts of the shells or the animal inside. These terms are defined in the glossary and are illustrated on the inside back cover.

The common (in bold type), scientific (in italics) and family (ending in idae) names are given for each shell. A common name might be considered a shell's nickname. Many times a shell is known by several common names, but recent authorities have designated one official common name for each shell. The first common and scientific name given in this guide are the official names recognized at the time of printing by Turgeon et al. (1988). Unofficially recognized common names are preceded by an asterisk; these include some designated by this author and others that had previously been described under a different name.

A scientific name may change as scientists discover more about a shell, decide it belongs in a different group or realize that the mollusk had previously been described under a different name. When someone discovers a shell for the first time, it is placed into a group of closely related shells called a genus. The scientific name is made up of that genus name, followed by a species name and the name of the person who first described it (the latter is not in italics). If the person's name appears in parentheses, the animal is now in a different genus than the one first proposed. The species name stays the same unless there is already a species by that name in the new genus.

• Using Shell Color in Identification

Most photographs in this guide are black and white because many shells are primarily white, and shell color can vary greatly. Often, shells washed onto the beach are bleached by the sun. Even during life, many shells vary in color — from white to yellow to purple. It is important to check the color description for each shell, but remember that some beach specimens may be faded or white instead of the color they are during life. Veteran shell collectors prefer good black-and-white photographs that show the details of the shell's surface sculpture and markings.

Old shells also present exceptions to the color descriptions. Over time, chemical changes occur in a shell's structure as compounds in the mud or seawater begin coating the crystals that comprise it. Iron oxide will turn shells a reddish brown or yellow. Iron sulfide will turn shells dark gray. Darker shells tend to be older. Color changes occur most quickly in shells sitting in the iron-rich water of a marsh. Also, the color of shells in a collection will disappear when exposed to sunlight over long periods of time.

** Unofficially recognized common names are preceded by an asterisk.*
◊ Shells with a photograph in the color section are preceded by a diamond.

Bivalves

ARK-SHAPED – arks (Arcidae)

white miniature ark

• **white miniature ark** *Barbatia domingensis* (Lamarck) (= *Acar domingensis*)
Description: (up to 1 1/4 inches but usually much smaller) Squarish, small, rough shell. Strong concentric ridges across weaker ribs. Long ligament. Long, almost straight hinge line with many tiny, chevron-shaped teeth. Bottom edge of shell not crenulated.
Color: White to yellowish white.
Habitat: Attaches to offshore jetties and shells or under rocks. Occasionally found on ocean beaches.
Range: North Carolina to Brazil.
Notes: Also called a **reticulate ark**. This bivalve has a bitter taste. It uses a byssus to attach to rocks and other objects.

white-bearded ark

• **white-bearded ark** *Barbatia candida* (Helbling)
Description: (1 inch) Similar to the **transverse ark** but less square. Front and back borders not parallel. Many fine, rough radial ribs crossed by concentric growth lines. Straight hinge line with many chevron-shaped teeth. Bottom edge crenulated from strong, exterior radial ribbing. Thin, shaggy periostracum when alive.
Color: White exterior. Yellowish brown periostracum when alive.
Habitat: Attaches to rocks. Occasionally found on ocean beaches.
Range: North Carolina to Brazil.
Notes: Also called a **bright ark**. It attaches to rocks by a byssus.

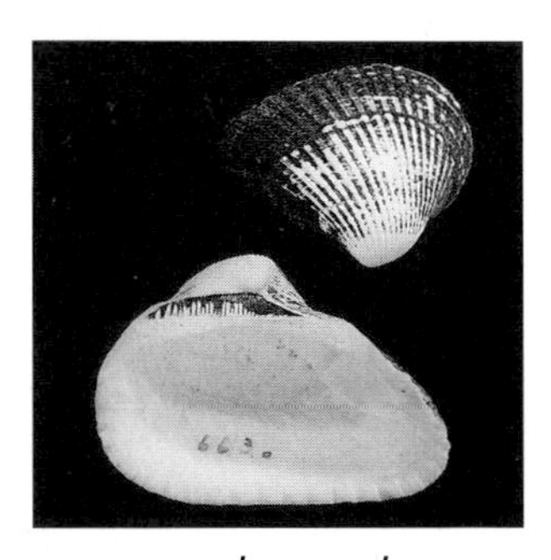

ponderous ark

• **ponderous ark** *Noetia ponderosa* (Say)
Description: (2 1/2 inches) Square, heavy shell. About 30 radial ribs cut by fine concentric lines but not beaded. Long hinge line narrower in center with many chevron-shaped teeth. Wide ligament cut by transverse lines (at 90-degree angle to length of ligament). Bottom edge not crenulated. Heavy, mossy periostracum when alive.
Color: White to yellowish white. Black periostracum when alive.
Habitat: Lives in inlets and offshore. Commonly found on ocean beaches.
Range: Virginia to Texas.
Notes: Its threadlike byssus is lost during larval stages. During its adult stage, it burrows in sand or mud rather than attaching to objects.

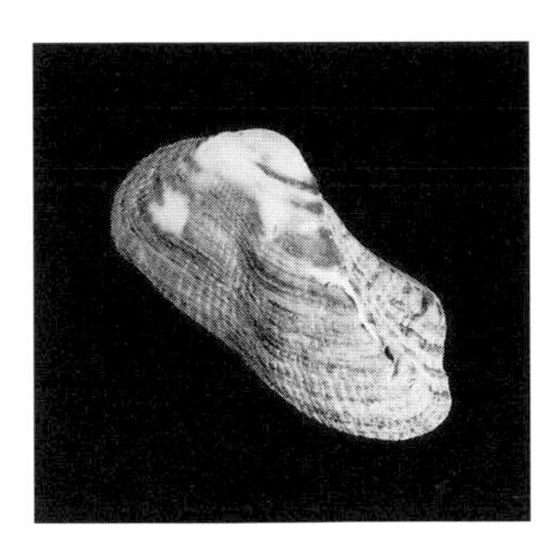

turkey wing

• turkey wing *Arca zebra* (Swainson)
Description: (3 1/2 inches) Elongate shell. Ribs at rear not beaded. Straight hinge line with many small, chevron-shaped teeth. Resembles **mossy ark** except bottom edge neither crenulated nor strongly concave. Live specimens often covered by a shaggy periostracum and/or encrusting organisms.
Color: Yellowish white or yellowish brown exterior with reddish brown zebra-stripe markings. Whitish to pale lavender interior.
Habitat: Attaches to shells or rocks on offshore fishing grounds or near-shore hard surfaces. Commonly found on ocean beaches.
Range: North Carolina to Brazil.
Notes: Also called a **zebra ark**. It attaches to objects by a byssus and is often difficult to see because of encrusting growths. Abbott (1974) reports it is served in Bermuda as part of a baked pie.

mossy ark

• mossy ark *Arca imbricata* Bruguière
Description: (2 1/2 inches) Similar shape to **turkey wing** but with weaker ribs. Ribs generally beaded. Part of lower edge strongly concave. Straight hinge line with many chevron-shaped teeth. Shaggy periostracum when alive.
Color: No exterior zebralike markings. White to pale lavender interior.
Habitat: See **turkey wing**.
Range: North Carolina to Brazil.
Notes: It attaches to objects by a byssus and is often difficult to see because of encrusting growths.

Adams' ark

• Adams' ark *Arcopsis adamsi* (Dall)
Description: (1/2 inch) Small, rectangular shell. Similar to **white miniature ark** but crisscross sculpturing less coarse and ligament only a small barlike area between beaks. Straight hinge line with many chevron-shaped teeth. Bottom edge smooth inside. Thin periostracum when living.
Color: White to yellowish white exterior. White interior. Pale brown periostracum when alive.
Habitat: Attaches to rocks. Occasionally found on ocean beaches.
Range: North Carolina to Brazil.
Notes: It attaches to the underside of rocks by a byssus.

cut-ribbed ark

• **cut-ribbed ark** *Anadara floridana* (Conrad)
Description: (4 1/2 inches) Large, sturdy, rectangular shell with 30 or more radial ribs, each with a groove running down the center. Prominent unbeaded ribs cut by fine concentric lines. Long, straight hinge line with many tiny, chevron-shaped teeth. Bottom edge crenulated. Mossy periostracum when alive.
Color: Exterior white. Periostracum brown when alive.
Habitat: Lives offshore. Occasionally found on ocean beaches.
Range: North Carolina to Texas.
Notes: Many of these arks were brought to shore by North Carolina's once-thriving **Atlantic calico scallop** fishery. Also see **ponderous ark *Notes***.

incongruous ark

• **incongruous ark** *Anadara brasiliana* (Lamarck)
Description: (2 1/2 inches) Inflated, rectangular shell with 26 to 28 strong radial ribs crossed by fine concentric lines. Grooves between ribs. Left valve larger than right. Ligament extends in front and back of beak. Straight hinge line with many chevron-shaped teeth, smaller toward the center. Bottom edge crenulated from strong exterior radial ribbing.
Color: White.
Habitat: Lives buried in sand. Commonly found on ocean beaches.
Range: North Carolina to Uruguay.
Notes: See **ponderous ark *Notes***.

blood ark

• **blood ark** *Anadara ovalis* (Bruguière) (= *Lunarca ovalis*)
Description: (2 1/4 inches) Oval-elliptical shell with 26 to 35 smooth radial ribs not crossed by strong bars (as in the **incongruous ark**). Ligament area in back of beak. Straight hinge line with chevron-shaped teeth extending only slightly beyond beak. Bottom edge crenulated from strong exterior radial ribbing.
Color: White exterior. Thick periostracum with greenish brown on lower portion when alive.
Habitat: Lives buried in sand and mud. Very commonly found on ocean beaches.
Range: Massachusetts to Texas.
Notes: Named for its red blood (most mollusks have bluish blood), it is sometimes called a **bloody clam**. Also see **ponderous ark *Notes***.

transverse ark

• **transverse ark** *Anadara transversa* (Say)
Description: (1 inch) Rectangular-shaped shell with 30 to 35 ribs. Ribs beaded (usually only on left valve) but not cut lengthwise by fine lines (as in the **cut-ribbed ark**). Beak near one end. Ligament extends in front and back of beak. Straight hinge line with many chevron-shaped teeth. Hairy periostracum when alive.
Color: White exterior and interior. Dark brown periostracum when alive.
Habitat: Attaches to rocks, shells and driftwood in sounds, inlets and offshore. Occasionally found on ocean beaches.
Range: Massachusetts to Texas.
Notes: Its periostracum is usually worn away except around edge.

ARK-SHAPED – bittersweets (Glycymerididae)

giant bittersweet

• **giant bittersweet** *Glycymeris americana* (DeFrance)
Description: (4 inches) Round, somewhat flat shell. Indistinct broad radial ribs sculptured with radiating scratches. Central beak. Long, curved hinge with 19 to 24 teeth. Scalloped margin. No pallial sinus. Velvety periostracum.
Color: Grayish tan exterior, mottled with yellowish brown. Dark brown periostracum.
Habitat: Lives offshore. Dense concentrations at 75-foot depths off Cape Fear. Commonly found on beaches near and south of Cape Fear. Occasionally netted as incidental catch by offshore fishing boats.
Range: North Carolina to Florida.
Notes: It has a bitter taste, as its name implies, so it cannot be considered for commercial harvest. It has a muscular foot.

comb bittersweet

• **comb bittersweet** *Glycymeris pectinata* (Gmelin)
Description: (3/4 inch) Round, somewhat flat shell. About 20 strong, smooth radial ribs crossed by tiny concentric lines. Curved hinge line with 22 to 25 teeth. No pallial sinus.
Color: Grayish white to yellowish white with yellow or brown splotches.
Habitat: Lives in shallow and offshore waters in sand or mud. Commonly found on ocean beaches.
Range: North Carolina to Brazil.
Notes: It has a bitter taste and a muscular foot. Two other species — the **spectral bittersweet**, *Glycymeris spectralis* Nicol, and the **wavy bittersweet**, *G. undata* (Linnaeus) — are found sporadically off the North Carolina coast.

ARK-SHAPED – nutclams (Nuculidae)

Atlantic nutclam

• **Atlantic nutclam** *Nucula proxima* Say
Description: (1/4 inch) Small, obliquely ovate shell with a shiny, smooth surface. Angular beak. Small, spoon-shaped depression under beak. Hinge line split into a 90-degree angle. Row of many crescent-shaped teeth on hinge. Inside of bottom edge crenulated.
Color: Exterior and interior iridescent white to gray.
Habitat: Lives in sand near shore in moderate-salinity estuaries and offshore in depths of more than 100 feet. Commonly washed onto ocean beaches.
Range: Nova Scotia, Canada, to Florida and Texas.
Notes: Also called a **common nutclam** and **near nut shell**. It is often eaten by fish and frequently found in the stomach of the sea star, *Astropecten articulatus*.

ARK-SHAPED – nutclams (Nuculanidae)

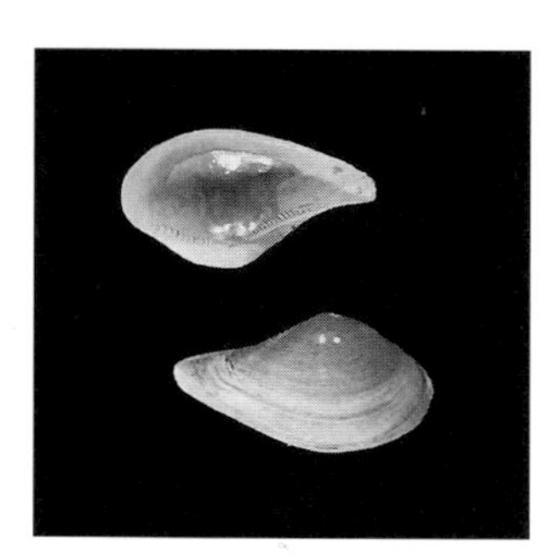

pointed nutclam

• **pointed nutclam** *Nuculana acuta* (Conrad)
Description: (3/8 inch or more) Small, thick, elliptical shell with one rounded end and one acutely pointed end. Top edge of shell slightly concave on the pointed end. Surface covered with evenly spaced and sized concentric ridges. Hinge line a wide obtuse angle. Row of many chevron-shaped teeth on hinge.
Color: Gray.
Habitat: Lives offshore on mud-sand bottoms in 50-foot depths. Occasionally found in high-salinity estuaries. Commonly washed onto ocean beaches.
Range: Cape Cod, Mass., to Texas and Brazil.
Notes: This species is often found in the stomach of the sea star, *Astropecten articulatus*.

file yoldia

• **file yoldia** *Yoldia limatula* (Say)
Description: (1 1/4 inches) Similar to the **pointed nutclam** except much larger with smooth rather than highly striated exterior.
Color: Exterior whitish to chestnut-gray to light greenish. Interior glossy white to tan.
Habitat: Lives off Beaufort Inlet at depths of 30 feet and more. Occasionally found on ocean beaches.
Range: Nova Scotia, Canada, to south of Beaufort Inlet, N.C.
Notes: This species is sometimes confused with the **short yoldia**, *Yoldia sapotilla* (Gould), which may have a similar habitat in North Carolina. The latter species is shorter and has a broadly rounded end instead of a pointed end.

COCKLE-SHAPED – cockles (Cardiidae)

spiny papercockle

• **spiny papercockle** *Papyridea soleniformis* (Bruguière)
Description: (1 1/2 inches) Thin, elliptical shell slightly elongated and not deeply cupped. Radial ribs with tiny spines near their ends. Prominent lateral teeth on hinge. No lunule or pallial sinus.
Color: Exterior and interior pinkish white, mottled with brownish orange and pink.
Habitat: Lives offshore. Its short siphons indicate that it lives just below mud surface. Occasionally found on ocean beaches from Cape Lookout south.
Range: North Carolina to Brazil.
Notes: Cockles are commonly eaten in Europe. The animal has a long, powerful foot that allows it to be active.

eggcockle

• **eggcockle** *Laevicardium laevigatum* (Linnaeus)
(= *L. multilineatum* Dall & Stimpson)
Description: (2 3/4 inches) Ovate to almost round, inflated, thin shell. Eggshell-like surface with light radial ribbing. No pallial sinus. Beak somewhat central. Prominent lateral teeth on hinge.
Color: Cream with brown tints.
Habitat: Lives in sand or mud, from shallow water to 150-foot depths offshore. Commonly found on ocean beaches.
Range: North Carolina to Brazil.
Notes: See **spiny papercockle** ***Notes***. This shell fades quickly to white on the beach.

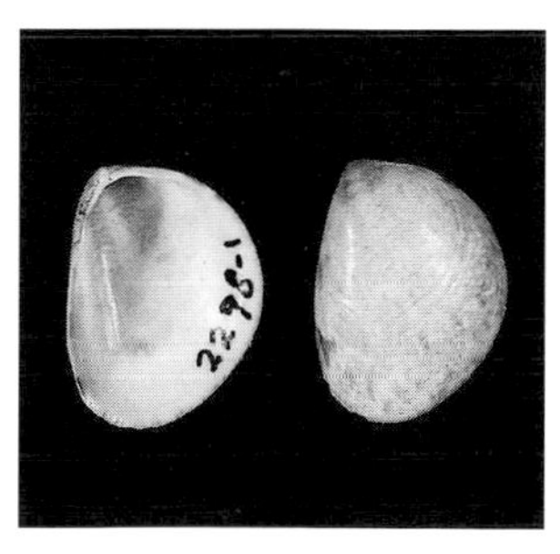

painted eggcockle

• **painted eggcockle** *Laevicardium pictum* (Ravenel)
Description: (1 inch) Small shell very similar to **Morton eggcockle** except more oblique in shape. Eggshell-like surface with light or no ribbing. No pallial sinus. Beak somewhat central. Prominent lateral teeth on hinge.
Color: Creamy white exterior with strong brown splotches or zigzagged bars. Yellow interior.
Habitat: Lives offshore. Rarely found on ocean beaches.
Range: North Carolina to Brazil.
Notes: It is sometimes called **Ravenel's eggcockle**. See **spiny papercockle** ***Notes***.

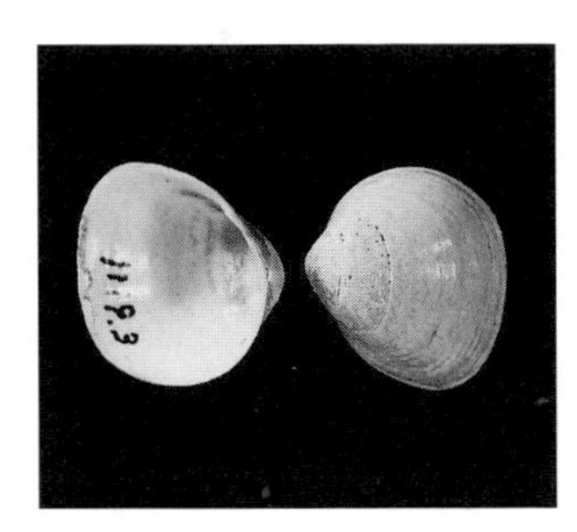
Morton eggcockle

• Morton eggcockle *Laevicardium mortoni* (Conrad)
Description: (3/4 inch) Small shell very similar to **painted eggcockle** except more rounded in shape. Eggshell-like surface with light or no ribbing. No pallial sinus. Beak somewhat central. Prominent lateral teeth on hinge.
Color: Yellowish white exterior, usually streaked with orange. Interior usually vivid yellow but fades quickly.
Habitat: Lives in sounds and estuaries. Occasionally found on sound beaches.
Range: Massachusetts to Guatemala.
Notes: See **spiny papercockle** ***Notes***.

Florida pricklycockle

• Florida pricklycockle *Trachycardium egmontianum* (Shuttleworth)
Description: (3 inches) Oval, inflated shell uniformly covered by ribs, each bearing raised scales over more than half its width. Beak somewhat central. Prominent lateral teeth on hinge. No pallial sinus. Bottom edge crenulated.
Color: Creamy white exterior, sometimes with brown or purple splotches. Interior salmon, vivid pink and purple.
Habitat: Lives in mouths of estuaries and shallow offshore waters. Occasionally found on sound and ocean beaches.
Range: North Carolina to Florida.
Notes: See **spiny papercockle** ***Notes***. It is often used in crafts.

yellow pricklycockle

• yellow pricklycockle *Trachycardium muricatum* (Linnaeus)
Description: (1 3/4 inches) Circular to oval, inflated shell with 30 to 40 radial ribs. Smooth ribs on center of shell; ribs on sides of shell with small, solid, nonscalelike spines over less than half the rib width. Bottom edge crenulated. Prominent lateral teeth on hinge.
Color: Creamy white exterior with brown or red splotches. White and yellow interior.
Habitat: Occasionally lives in estuaries. Found on ocean beaches. More common south of Morehead City.
Range: North Carolina to Argentina.
Notes: See **spiny papercockle** ***Notes***.

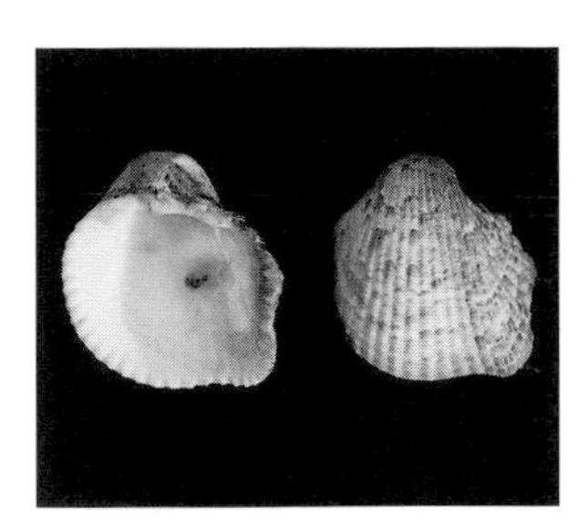

Atlantic strawberry-cockle

• **Atlantic strawberry-cockle** *Americardia media* (Linnaeus)
Description: (1 1/2 inches) Thickish shell with squared-off sides. Strong radial ribs with no spines or elevated scales. Beak somewhat central. Strong angle from beak to bottom edge. Prominent lateral teeth on hinge. Smooth interior. No pallial sinus. Bottom edge crenulated.
Color: Creamy white exterior with irregular transverse rows of reddish brown spots. Purplish spots sometimes in interior.
Habitat: Lives offshore. Occasionally found on ocean beaches.
Range: North Carolina to Brazil.
Notes: See **spiny papercockle** *Notes*.

Atlantic giant-cockle

• **Atlantic giant-cockle** *Dinocardium robustum* (Lightfoot)
Description: (4 1/2 inches) Circular to ovate shell, thick and deeply inflated. Radial ribs rough but no spines or elevated scales. Beak somewhat central. Prominent lateral teeth on hinge. Ribbed interior. No pallial sinus.
Color: Yellowish white to pale rosy brown exterior with bands of reddish brown or purplish spots. Rose to brown interior, paler toward front and darker toward rear.
Habitat: Lives in sounds and shallow offshore waters. Commonly found on sound and ocean beaches.
Range: Virginia to Belize.
Notes: Its reddish meat makes an excellent chowder. It is the largest cockle on the Atlantic coast.

COCKLE-SHAPED – carditas (Carditidae)

threetooth carditid

• **threetooth carditid** *Pleuromeris tridentata* (Say) (= *Venericardia tridentata*)
Description: (1/4 inch) Small, chunky triangular shell of equal height and length. Strongly beaded radial ribs. Central beak. One strong, triangular cardinal hinge tooth under beak of the right valve; two slightly smaller diverging cardinal teeth on the left valve. Inside edge of shell strongly crenulated. No pallial sinus.
Color: Cream to pinkish gray exterior. Creamy white to red interior.
Habitat: Lives on sandy and shelly bottoms offshore to about 75-foot depths and in high-salinity estuaries. Commonly found on ocean beaches south of Cape Hatteras.
Range: Cape Hatteras, N.C., to Florida.
Notes: The holes on the shell in the photograph are the result of predatory activity by a moonsnail.

flattened carditid

• **flattened carditid** *Pleuromeris perplana* (Conrad)
(= *Venericardia perplana*)
Description: (3/8 inch) Small, somewhat flattened, obliquely oval or triangular shell. Beak back of center. Strong, broad, rough radial ribs that curve toward front of the shell. Ribs sometimes beaded. Hinge teeth similar to **threetooth carditid**. Inside edge of shell crenulated. No pallial sinus.
Color: Creamish exterior with occasional pink concentric bands. Cream interior with occasional pink to strong violet.
Habitat: Lives in 20- to 30-foot depths south of Cape Hatteras. Occasionally found on ocean beaches.
Range: North Carolina to Florida.

OYSTER-SHAPED – wing-oysters (Pteriidae)

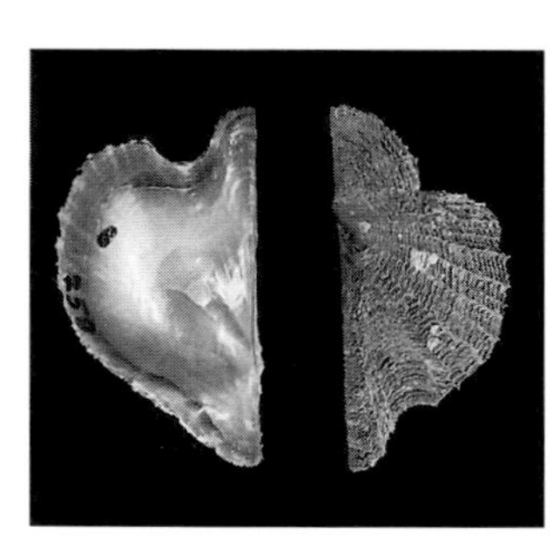

Atlantic wing-oyster

◊ • **Atlantic wing-oyster** *Pteria colymbus* (Röding)
Description: (3 3/4 inches) Triangular shell with winglike extension from the straight hinge line. Other side rounded. Hinge longest part of shell with few teeth. Wrinkled exterior.
Color: Brownish purple exterior. Iridescent interior.
Habitat: Lives in sounds and offshore, commonly attached to shells, rocks, sea whips or floating docks. Often found on sea whips washed ashore after storms. Occasionally found on sound and ocean beaches.
Range: North Carolina to Brazil.
Notes: Closely related to pearl oysters, its pearls are rare and usually too small to be valuable. The mantle produces mother-of-pearl, or nacre. Pearls form when a grain of sand or other particle enters the shell and is coated with layers of nacre.

Atlantic pearl-oyster

• **Atlantic pearl-oyster** *Pinctada imbricata* Röding
(= *P. radiata* Leach)
Description: (1 1/2 inches) Nearly circular shell with long, flattened hinge line forming a winglike extension. Small, flattened ligament in center of hinge line. Byssal notch below small triangular ear of the right valve. Thin-shelled and brittle. Thin, scaly, concentric spines sometimes on periostracum.
Color: Exterior yellow or green with dark radial streaks or dark brownish purple with white streaks. Pearly interior.
Description: Attaches to sargassum or other drifting objects. Often found on ocean beaches where sargassum washes ashore.
Range: North Carolina to Florida, Texas and Brazil.
Notes: See **Atlantic wing-oyster** ***Notes***.

OYSTER-SHAPED – edible oysters (Ostreidae)

eastern oyster

• **eastern oyster** *Crassostrea virginica* (Gmelin)
Description: (8 1/2 inches) Shell elongate and usually heavy. Shaped by surface to which it attaches (usually another oyster). Lacks pimplelike depressions on either side of hinge and lacks hinge teeth. Prominent muscle scar inside. Lower valve cemented to another hard surface.
Color: Dirty white to dark gray or purple exterior. Grayish white interior with dark purple muscle scar.
Habitat: Lives in intertidal areas near mouths of sounds and estuaries. Common on sound and ocean beaches.
Range: New Brunswick, Canada, to the Gulf of Mexico.
Notes: The **eastern oyster** is an important fishery in North Carolina's estuarine waters. A hermaphrodite, it may change sex several times during life. It sheds sperm and eggs into water, where fertilization and development take place. Larvae swim freely for about two weeks, cement to a hard object and remain for life. For a brief period after attachment, they are called "spat." Thousands of spat have been recorded attached to one oyster shell, but generally only one or two will survive. The mantle does not produce nacre, or mother-of-pearl, so pearls found in them are not valuable. They are called **coon oysters** when they grow long, narrow and thin-shelled from crowded conditions in intertidal areas.

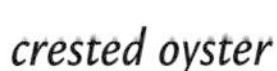

crested oyster

• **crested oyster** *Ostreola equestris* (Say)
(= *Ostrea equestris*)
Description: (2 inches) Shell very similar to **eastern oyster** except more round than elongate with small pimplelike depressions on either side of hinge.
Color: Brownish gray exterior. Greenish gray interior. Muscle scar generally not colored.
Habitat: Lives in high-salinity areas, such as mouths of sounds, estuaries and offshore. Common on sound and ocean beaches.
Range: Virginia to Argentina.
Notes: Rarely used commercially, it is only an incidental catch from high-salinity sounds or inlets. It has an excellent taste and is closely related to commercial oysters in Europe and on the northwestern U.S. coast. Unlike the **eastern oyster**, which releases eggs and sperm into the water, sperm enter the female's mantle cavity through her siphon. The fertilized eggs of the **crested oyster** incubate in the mantle until they hatch and are released into surrounding waters. In both species, the young develop similarly, and sex reversal is common.

sponge oyster

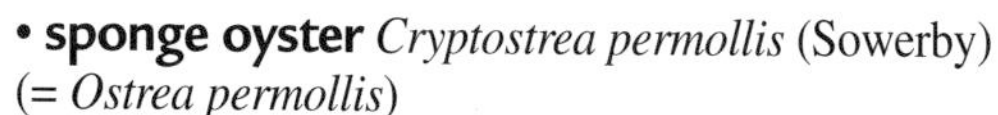

• **sponge oyster** *Cryptostrea permollis* (Sowerby) (= *Ostrea permollis*)
Description: (2 inches) Similar to **crested oyster**. Small, roundish shell with pointed or twisted beak. Both valves flat. Wrinkled surface somewhat soft. No hinge teeth. One muscle scar. Ligament often angled down from the beak. Some round pimplelike depressions on inner edges. Lower valve cemented to another hard surface.
Color: Yellowish orange exterior with a silky sheen. White to dark gray interior.
Habitat: Lives offshore, embedded in round sponge masses (*Stellata* species) in 80- to 100-foot depths south of Cape Lookout. Also reported to live under rock slabs. Found by scuba divers and netted as incidental catch by fishing trawlers. Sponge masses occasionally washed onto ocean beaches.
Range: North Carolina to Florida and West Indies.
Notes: Related to the **crested oyster**, females incubate the young.

frond oyster

• **frond oyster** *Dendostrea frons* (Linnaeus) (= *Ostrea frons* or *Lopha frons*)
Description: (1 1/2 inches) Irregular radial ridges on surface create sharply scalloped edges. Series of clasping projections on one of the radial ridges on lower valve. No hinge teeth. Pimplelike depressions on the inside edges of valve.
Color: Red to purplish brown.
Habitat: Lives offshore, usually attached to sea whips. Collected by scuba divers at 100-foot depths in Cape Fear region. Rarely found on ocean beaches.
Range: North Carolina to Florida and Brazil.
Notes: Also called a **coon oyster**. It attaches to sea whips with clasping projections.

OYSTER-SHAPED – kittenpaws (Plicatulidae)

Atlantic kittenpaw

• **Atlantic kittenpaw** *Plicatula gibbosa* Lamarck
Description: (1 1/2 inches) Small, thick, fan-shaped shell resembling the outstretched paw of a kitten. Six or seven rounded radial ribs or folds. Two strong hinge teeth in upper valve fit into sockets of the lower valve. One muscle scar. Lower valve cemented or showing signs of having been cemented to a hard surface.
Color: Whitish gray exterior with reddish brown lines. Whitish interior.
Habitat: Lives offshore, cemented to shell or rock. Commonly found on ocean beaches.

Continued on upper right

Continued from lower left

Range: North Carolina to Argentina.
Notes: Its colors fade quickly, so most beach specimens are dull white.

OYSTER-SHAPED – jewelboxes (Chamidae)

leafy jewelbox

• **leafy jewelbox** *Chama macerophylla* Gmelin
Description: (1 1/2 inches) Solid oysterlike shell with leafy, ruffly and sometimes spiny sculpture. Hinge teeth. Beak points toward right. Lower valve cupped and attached to hard surface. Upper valve a semiflat lid for lower valve.
Color: Whitish exterior and interior with variable but often brilliant colors such as yellow, purple, orange and pink.
Habitat: Lives offshore, attached to shells and rocks. Rarely found on ocean beaches.
Range: North Carolina to Brazil.
Notes: The "ruffles" grow larger in quiet waters.

corrugate jewelbox

• **corrugate jewelbox** *Chama congregata* Conrad
Description: (1 1/4 inches) Small, heavy shell irregularly oval or rounded. Surface sculpture of low, wavy radial cords or ridges. Hinge teeth. Beak points toward right. Lower valve quite cupped and attached to hard surface. Upper valve a semiflat lid.
Color: White exterior usually mottled with brown or reddish purple. Interior usually reddish.
Habitat: Lives offshore, attached to shells or rocks. Occasionally found on ocean beaches.
Range: North Carolina to Brazil.
Notes: It is often covered with algae.

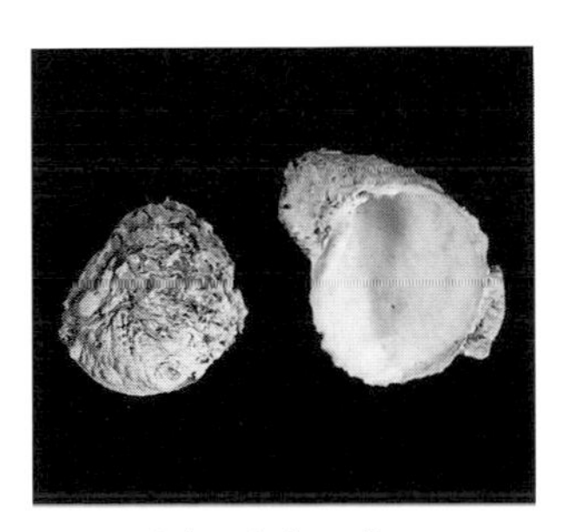

Atlantic jewelbox

• **Atlantic jewelbox** *Pseudochama radians* (Lamarck)
Description: (2 1/2 inches) Almost a mirror image of **leafy jewelbox** with beak pointing left. Generally larger than other jewelboxes listed here. Hinge teeth. Lower valve deeply cupped and attached to hard surface. Upper valve a semiflat lid.
Color: Exterior dull white to dull, rusty red. Whitish interior often tinged with brown.
Habitat: Lives in deep offshore waters, attached to shells and rocks. Occasionally found on ocean beaches.
Range: North Carolina to Brazil.
Notes: Also called a **false jewelbox**.

Florida spiny jewelbox

• **Florida spiny jewelbox** *Arcinella cornuta* Conrad
Description: (2 inches) Thick shell pitted with six to eight strong radial ribs bearing tubular spines. Surface between ribs beaded. Curved beak. Hinge teeth. Both valves deeply cupped. Prominent lunule. Adults not cemented to any hard surface.
Color: White exterior. White interior with some pinkish red.
Habitat: Lives offshore. Occasionally found on ocean beaches.
Range: North Carolina to Texas.
Notes: The young attach to bits of shell or rock. Later they become free and lie on the bottom, but the smooth attachment scar remains visible in front of the beak on the right valve.

OYSTER-SHAPED – jingles (Anomiidae)

common jingle

• **common jingle** *Anomia simplex* d'Orbigny
Description: (1 1/2 inches) Irregularly oval or round shell, thin and almost translucent. Top valve convex. Bottom valve flat and fragile with a slotlike hole near the hinge. One large and several small muscle scars close together. No hinge teeth.
Color: Exterior top (convex) valve whitish to yellow-orange to silvery black. Translucent bottom (flat) valve. Pearly interior.
Habitat: Lives from the low tide line to shallow offshore waters, attached but not cemented to rocks, oysters and other hard surfaces. Commonly found on sound and ocean beaches.
Range: New York to the West Indies.
Notes: A large byssus protrudes through the hole in its lower valve and attaches to other objects. The top shell often takes the appearance of the shell it attaches to. These shells are sometimes strung up and used as wind chimes.

prickly jingle

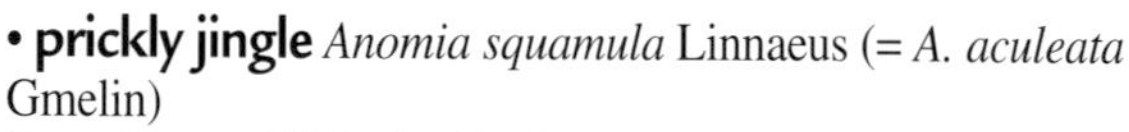

• **prickly jingle** *Anomia squamula* Linnaeus (= *A. aculeata* Gmelin)
Description: (3/4 inch) Similar to **common jingle** but much smaller with tiny spines on upper valve. One large muscle scar above two smaller muscle scars on bottom valve.
Color: Exterior opaque whitish tan. Interior shiny purplish white.
Habitat: Lives in high-salinity estuaries and offshore waters, attached but not cemented to hard surfaces such as stones, shells or floating objects (buoys). Occasionally found on ocean beaches.
Range: Labrador, Canada, to North Carolina.
Notes: See **common jingle** ***Notes***.

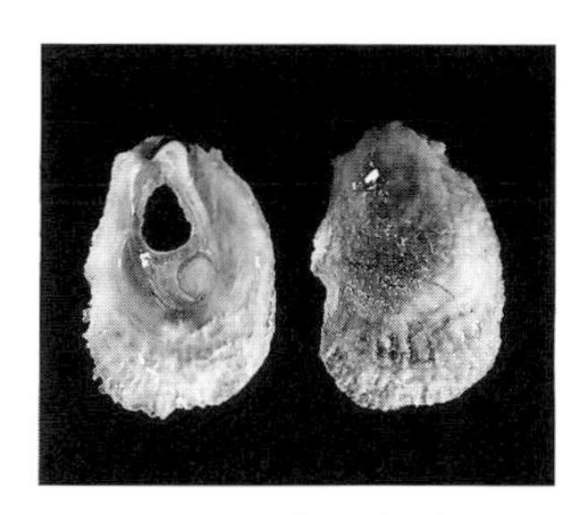
Atlantic falsejingle

• **Atlantic falsejingle** *Pododesmus rudis* (Broderip)
Description: (1 1/4 inches) Oval shell. Surface roughened by fine irregular riblets, primarily near valve edges. One valve seems cemented to the bottom with a large hole for the byssus. One large and one small muscle scar on inside of the other valve.
Color: Cream exterior. Interior may have some brownish purple near the muscle scars.
Habitat: Lives offshore. Found attached to arks and bittersweets at 100-foot depths in the Cape Fear area. Collected by scuba divers from metal rubble of sunken shipwrecks south of Cape Lookout. Rarely found on ocean beaches.
Range: North Carolina to Texas and Brazil.
Notes: Also called a **false jingleshell.**

SCALLOP-SHAPED – thorny-oysters (Spondylidae)

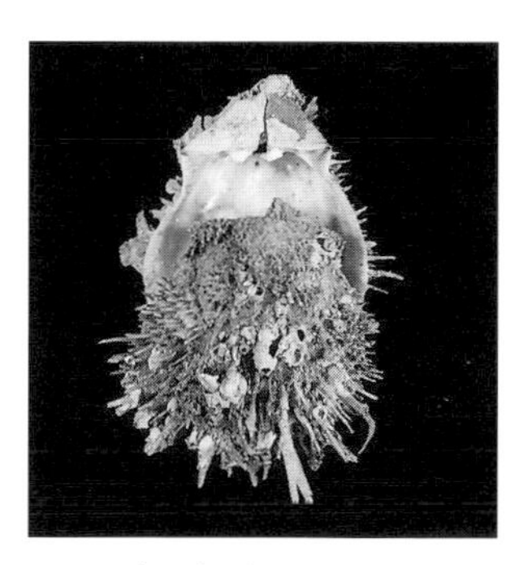
Atlantic thorny-oyster

◊ • **Atlantic thorny-oyster** *Spondylus americanus* Hermann
Description: (4 inches) Large, thick-shelled, broadly ovate shell with long, thin spines. Spines short or grow more than 2 inches long. Resembles a jewelbox except this shell has ears like a scallop, a ball-and-socket hinge and a central ligament.
Color: White or cream exterior with yellow to pink, red or purple. White interior.
Habitat: Lives on rocks and shipwrecks in offshore waters more than 60 feet deep.
Range: Cape Hatteras, N.C., to Florida, Texas and Brazil.
Notes: It attaches by its right valve to hard surfaces. The spines grow longer in quiet water.

SCALLOP-SHAPED – scallops (Pectinidae)

lions-paw scallop

◊ • **lions-paw scallop** *Nodipecten nodosus* (Linnaeus)
(= *Lyropecten nodosus*)
Description: (4 3/4 inches) Large, heavy, scallop-shaped shell resembling the paw of a large cat. Large radial ribs roughened with large nodules. Valves almost flat and equal in size. Hinge line with ears.
Color: Exterior orange, red, brown or black. Glossy interior, usually pinkish orange.
Habitat: Lives offshore. Rarely found on ocean beaches.
Range: North Carolina to Brazil.
Notes: Reportedly delicious, this species was common in some catches of the **Atlantic calico scallop** fishery.

rough scallop

◊ • **rough scallop** *Aequipecten muscosus* (W. Wood)
(= *Chlamys muscosus*)
Description: (1 3/4 inches) Small, scallop-shaped shell. About 20 strong ribs with many erect scales or small spines near the margin. Hinge line with ears.
Color: Pink to dark red exterior, occasionally mixed with other colors — sometimes bright lemon-yellow.
Habitat: Lives offshore. Rarely found on ocean beaches.
Range: North Carolina to the West Indies.
Notes: It was frequently netted as incidental catch in the **Atlantic calico scallop** fishery.

sea scallop

• **sea scallop** *Placopecten magellanicus* (Gmelin)
Description: (6 1/2 inches) Large, smooth shell. Hinge line with ears. Many fine concentric lines. Lower valve almost flat, and upper valve only slightly inflated.
Color: Exterior of top valve reddish brown, sometimes rayed; bottom valve glossy pinkish white. Whitish interior.
Habitat: Lives offshore. Might occur on ocean beaches north of Cape Hatteras.
Range: Labrador, Canada, to Cape Hatteras, N.C.
Notes: Also called the **Atlantic deep-sea scallop**, it was fished commercially for its delicious meat. It is much larger than other North Carolina scallops. Specimens from Virginia and New Jersey were once common in piles near commercial scallop-shucking plants in Carteret County. Early Native Americans used the valves as dishes. Today, tourists often purchase them to use as ashtrays.

Ravenel scallop

• **Ravenel scallop** *Pecten raveneli* Dall
Description: (2 3/4 inches) Hinge line with ears. Lower valve very cupped; upper valve flat. Smooth, radial ribs with wide spaces between them.
Color: Pinkish, purple or sometimes yellow. Upper valve darker with irregular dark markings.
Habitat: Lives offshore.
Range: North Carolina to the West Indies.
Notes: This scallop was once mistaken by shellfishers as a sick **Atlantic calico scallop** because of its flat upper valve. Today, it is a popular shell among tourists.

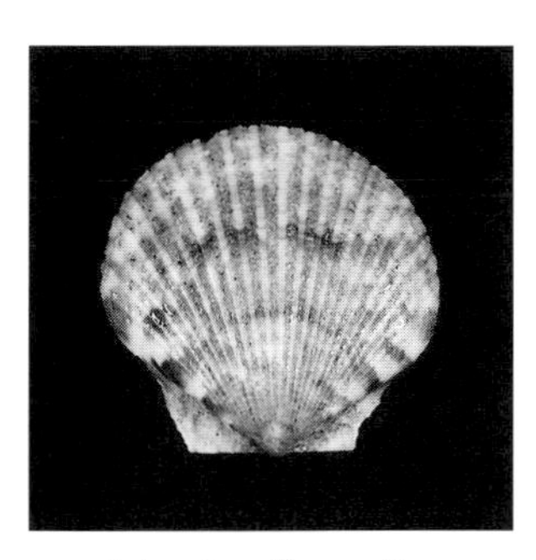

Atlantic calico scallop

• **Atlantic calico scallop** *Argopecten gibbus* (Linnaeus)
Description: (3 inches) Similar in shape and sculpturing to the **Atlantic bay scallop**. Both valves cupped. Hinge line with ears. About 20 radial ribs sometimes roughened by growth lines.
Color: Exterior of upper (left) valve dark yellow or pink with striking combinations of red in stripes or blotches. Lower (right) valve whitish with small reddish or purple spots. White interior, often with brown patches on ears and top edge.
Habitat: Lives only in ocean, east of Cape Lookout and southwest of Beaufort Inlet in 100-foot depths. Commonly found on sound and ocean beaches.
Range: Delaware to Brazil.
Notes: It is occasionally fished commercially and popular among tourists.

Atlantic bay scallop

• **Atlantic bay scallop** *Argopecten irradians concentricus* (Say)
Description: (3 1/2 inches) Similar in shape and sculpturing to **Atlantic calico scallop** (note color differences). Both valves cupped. Fifteen to 22 smooth radial ribs.
Color: Upper valve gray, brown or blackish, sometimes with only the upper surface of ribs colored. Lower valve usually with less color than the upper valve.
Habitat: In North Carolina, lives only in sounds and estuaries.
Range: Massachusetts to Mexico.
Notes: A major commercial fishery in North Carolina sounds and estuaries, it can be collected by dragging a rake or small oyster dredge through eelgrass beds. The loss of eelgrass, however, has caused a decline in the bay scallop. It is one of three subspecies of bay scallop recognized in the North Atlantic from Massachusetts to Mexico; see Abbott (1974) and Walter (1969) for detailed differences. The two other subspecies are:

(1) **Northern Atlantic bay scallop**, *Argopecten irradians irradians* (Lamarck), found from Cape Cod, Mass., to Maryland. It has flatter, thinner valves than the one in North Carolina waters.

(2) **Texas bay scallop**, *Argopecten irradians amplicostatus* (Dall), found from Galveston, Texas, to the Mexican coast. It has thicker, more convex valves and fewer radial ribs (13 to 16) than the one in North Carolina waters.

SCALLOP-SHAPED – fileclams (Limidae)

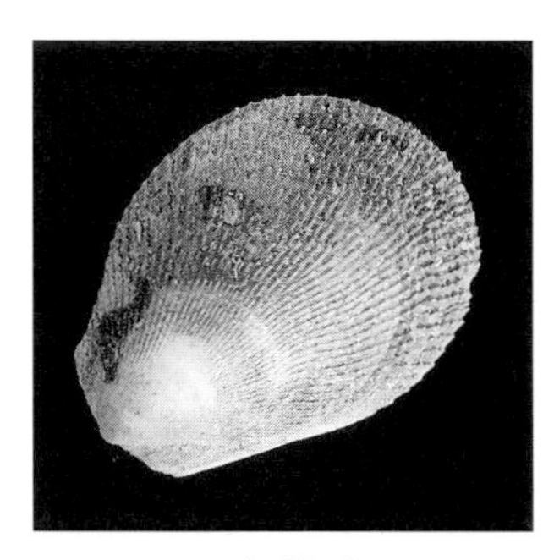

rough fileclam

• **rough fileclam** *Lima scabra* (Born)
Description: (2 5/8 inches) Compressed, oval-shaped shell with small ears. Coarse radial ribbing resembles narrow roof shingling. Gap on one side of shell. Long tentacles when alive.
Color: Whitish exterior but thin, brown periostracum lends it a brownish color. White interior. Bright orange-red mantle and tentacles when alive.
Habitat: Lives offshore, attached to rocks and shipwrecks. Collected by scuba divers at depths greater than 75 feet.
Range: Cape Lookout, N.C., to Florida, Texas and Brazil.
Notes: Also called a **rough lima** or **Atlantic rough file shell.** The animal attaches to surfaces by its byssus but also swims in a manner similar to scallops by opening and closing its valves. Another form of this species, *Lima scabra tenera* Sowerby, is smoother and has finer, more numerous ribs.

Antillean fileclam

• **Antillean fileclam** *Lima pellucida* C.B. Adams (= *Limaria pellucida*)
Description: (3/4 inch) Oval-elongate, inflated shell. Many fine radial ribs of uneven sizes on surface. Small, straight hinge line. Ears almost equal in length. Under ears, long, narrow gape in the front and large gape in the back. Thin-shelled.
Color: Translucent to yellowish white.
Habitat: Lives in high-salinity estuaries, such as Bogue Sound, Newport River and North River, usually attached to the bottom. Also found offshore at depths close to 100 feet.
Range: North Carolina to Florida, Texas and Brazil.
Notes: Also called an **Antillean lima** or **inflated file shell.** It is known to surround itself with a nest of byssal threads. It is able to swim in a manner similar to scallops.

MUSSEL-SHAPED – mussels (Mytilidae)

• **blue mussel** *Mytilus edulis* Linnaeus
Description: (2 1/2 inches) Elongate, triangular shell generally twice as long as high. No radial ribs, but many fine concentric lines. Beak located at one end of shell. Small teeth just under beak. Shiny periostracum.
Color: Bluish black exterior. White interior with lavender near edges. Young specimens sometimes greenish and/or rayed.

Continued on upper right

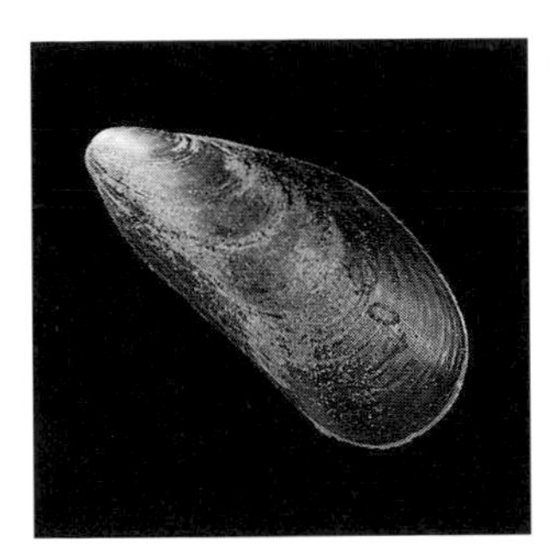

blue mussel

Continued from lower left

Habitat: Lives offshore and in mouths of estuaries, attached to rocks, shells, jetties and pilings. Common on ocean beaches north of Cape Hatteras; adults rarely found south of Cape Hatteras.
Range: Arctic Ocean to South Carolina.
Notes: This is a popular edible mussel in Europe. It is smaller than most of North Carolina's other edible bivalves, but it has a large potential for advanced aquaculture. It withstands waves by attaching to hard surfaces by a tough, elastic byssus. Its streamlined shape allows water to glide by with little resistance.

northern horsemussel

• **northern horsemussel** *Modiolus modiolus* (Linnaeus)
Description: (4 1/2 inches) Elongate shell generally more than twice as long as high. Coarse concentric growth lines. Occasionally some radiating lines. Beak points toward one end. No hinge teeth. Leathery periostracum with some hairs.
Color: No chestnut-colored splotch on lower front area as in **American horsemussel**. Pale purple to rose-white exterior. Brownish black periostracum.
Habitat: Lives offshore, attached to rocks, shells or jetties. Commonly found on ocean beaches.
Range: Arctic Sea to Venezuela.
Notes: This is the largest and most common mussel of New England, but it is not good to eat. It withstands waves by attaching to objects with a tough, elastic byssus. Its streamlined shape allows water to glide by with little resistance.

American horsemussel

• **American horsemussel** *Modiolus americanus* (Leach)
Description: (2 1/4 inches) Elongate, oblong, inflated shell. One end narrower than the other. Resembles **northern horsemussel** but not as large and heavy. No ribs on smooth exterior, only concentric growth lines. Rolled, pearly area just below its ligament. Stringlike, hairy periostracum.
Color: Brown exterior, sometimes with reddish purple or pink. Deep chestnut-colored splotch in lower front area. Grayish white or reddish interior. Light brown periostracum.
Habitat: Lives in sounds and offshore, attached to rocks, shells and jetties. Commonly found on ocean beaches after storms.
Range: North Carolina to Brazil.
Notes: This species is also called **tulip mussel** because of the reddish color on its shell when dead.

false horsemussel

* • **false horsemussel** *Modiolus modiolus squamosus* Beauperthuy
Description: (2 1/4 inches) Similar to **northern** and **American horsemussels**. Lacks the rolled, pearly area below its ligament that is reported in the **American horsemussel**. Flat triangular hairs on periostracum.
Color: Similar to **northern** and **American horsemussels**. Chestnut splotch on lower front area not as showy as on the **American horsemussel**.
Habitat: Believed to be common on jetties in Bogue Sound.
Range: North Carolina to Venezuela.
Notes: The commonness of this subspecies in North Carolina has yet to be determined.

giant datemussel

• **giant datemussel** *Lithophaga antillarum* (d'Orbigny)
Description: (3 1/4 inches) Cigar-shaped shell with rounded ends. Sculptured with many light, irregular, vertical lines. No hinge teeth.
Color: Light yellow-brown exterior. Brown periostracum.
Habitat: Lives offshore (mainly off Cape Lookout), inside lumps of coral.
Range: North Carolina to Brazil.
Notes: Young attach to rocks by a byssus. Adults bore into limestone and other soft rocks.

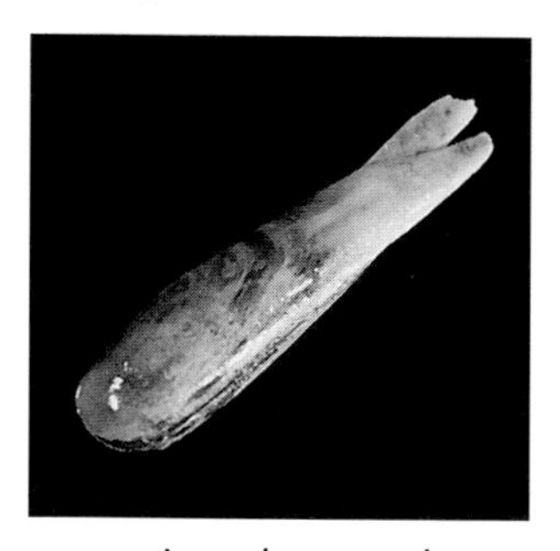

scissor datemussel

• **scissor datemussel** *Lithophaga aristata* (Dillwyn)
Description: (1 1/4 inches) Elongate, narrow, cigar-shaped shell. Extended ends like crossed fingers, the end of a small pair of scissors or sometimes an open bird's beak.
Color: Light brown exterior generally covered by white calcareous deposit.
Habitat: Lives offshore, inside coral lumps, soft rock and thick shells.
Range: North Carolina to Venezuela.
Notes: It bores into rocks, shells and wood by rotating its shell and using secretions to soften coral and limestone. It breathes and feeds through siphons that it extends outside of its burrow.

mahogany datemussel

• mahogany datemussel *Lithophaga bisulcata* (d'Orbigny)
Description: (1 1/4 inches) Cigar-shaped shell. Exterior surface divided by a wide oblique line from beak area to end of shell. Ends not crossed. One end bluntly pointed. Calcareous deposits on surface.
Color: Light brown exterior with white calcareous deposits.
Habitat: Lives in sounds and offshore, inside coral and soft rock.
Range: North Carolina to Brazil.
Notes: See **scissor datemussel** ***Notes***.

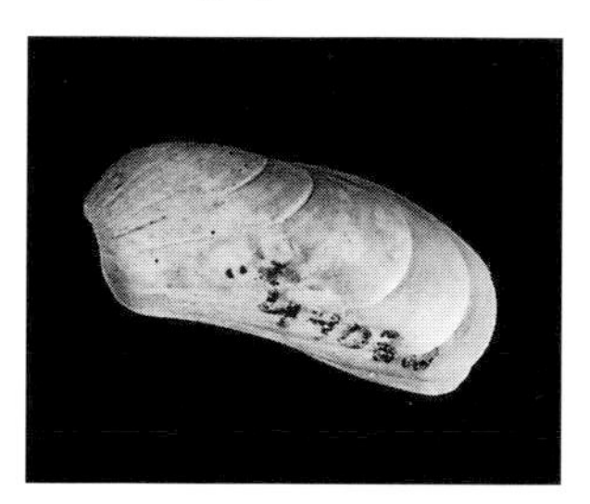
cinnamon mussel

• cinnamon mussel *Botula fusca* (Gmelin)
Description: (1/2 inch) Small, cigar-shaped shell with concave lower edge. Strong concentric growth lines. Beak at one end sometimes appears to form a hook. No hinge teeth. Shiny periostracum.
Color: Grayish brown to dark chestnut brown.
Habitat: Lives offshore, inside rocks and shells.
Range: North Carolina to Brazil.
Notes: See **scissor datemussel** ***Notes***.

scorched mussel

• scorched mussel *Brachidontes exustus* (Linnaeus)
(= *Hormomya exusta*)
Description: (1 1/2 inches) Small, elongate, fan-shaped shell. Narrow end not strongly hooked. Axial ribs on the surface. Beak toward one end. One to four small hinge teeth.
Color: Brownish yellow-gray exterior. Whitish to shiny purplish gray interior, splotched with reddish purple. Yellowish brown periostracum.
Habitat: Lives in estuaries, often attached to oysters or other shells or rocks.
Range: North Carolina to Venezuela.
Notes: It is commonly washed ashore still attached to shells, rocks and seaweed.

hooked mussel

• hooked mussel *Ischadium recurvum* (Rafinesque)
(= *Brachidontes recurvus*)
Description: (1 3/4 inches) Curved, triangular shell with strong radial ribs that branch near one end. Narrow end of shell strongly hooked. Beak near one end. A few toothlike crenulations on hinge.
Color: Dark grayish black exterior. Polished purple interior with white at margins.
Habitat: Lives in estuaries, often attached to oysters or other shells and rocks.
Range: Massachusetts to the West Indies.
Notes: Also called a **bent mussel**.

ribbed mussel

• **ribbed mussel** *Geukensia demissa* (Dillwyn)
Description: (5 1/4 inches) Elongate, obliquely oval shell with one end narrower than the other. Strong, heavy radial ribs sometimes branch. Toothless hinge.
Color: Dark brown to purple exterior. Blue-white interior. Olive brown to dark brown periostracum.
Habitat: Lives in large groups in muddy intertidal areas of brackish marshes. Often found among the roots of the marsh cord grass, *Spartina*.
Range: Nova Scotia, Canada, to Florida.
Notes: It attaches to cord grass stems and other substrates by its byssus. It grows well in polluted areas.

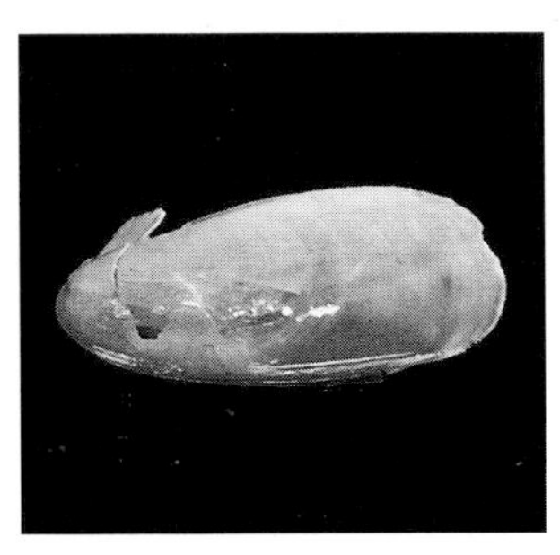

Atlantic papermussel

• **Atlantic papermussel** *Amygdalum papyrium* (Conrad)
Description: (1 inch) Elongate, fragile shell generally more than twice as long as high. Smooth exterior with fine concentric growth lines.
Color: Shiny light blue and tan exterior with brown cobwebby design. Iridescent interior. Light green periostracum.
Habitat: Lives in estuaries and offshore.
Range: Maryland to Texas.
Notes: It uses its byssal threads to build nests.

MUSSEL-SHAPED – gastrochaenas (Gastrochaenidae)

Atlantic rocellaria

• **Atlantic rocellaria** *Gastrochaena hians* (Gmelin)
(= *Rocellaria hians*)
Description: (5/8 inch) Elliptical shell. Resembles a mussel or piddock with beak close to the front end. Large gape just behind beak. Thin-shelled. Small hinge teeth.
Color: Chalky white exterior. White interior.
Habitat: Lives offshore burrowed inside coral rock. Occasionally lives in high-salinity estuarine areas such as Wreck Point and Cape Lookout. Collected by scuba divers at a 70-foot depth off Wrightsville Beach (burrowed into rock).
Range: North Carolina to Brazil.
Notes: Also called an **Atlantic gastrochaena**. This species forms burrows in coral rock that are flasklike and lined with a calcareous substance. It has long siphons.

PENSHELL-SHAPED – penshells (Pinnidae)

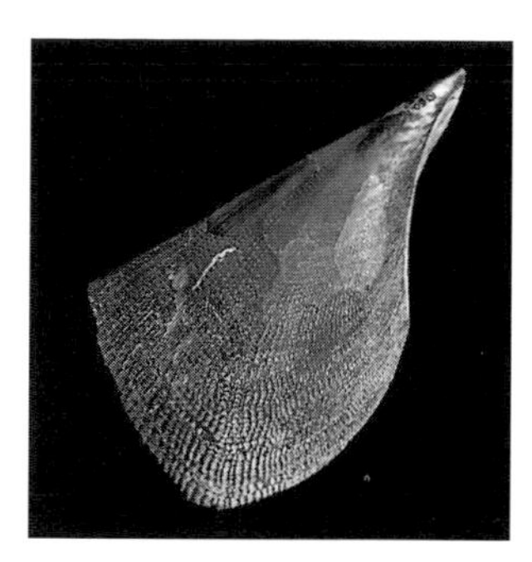
sawtooth penshell

• **sawtooth penshell** *Atrina serrata* (Sowerby)
Description: (10 inches) Large and fan-shaped shell with one side straight and the other rounded. Fragile and scaly. About 30 ribs covered with small spines.
Color: Green to yellowish brown exterior. Pearly interior.
Habitat: Lives offshore in sandy mud. Commonly found on ocean beaches after winter storms.
Range: North Carolina to Colombia.
Notes: Brittleness makes this shell difficult to keep in collections. Its edible meat is considered valuable in some parts of the world. Penshell muscle is sometimes sold as "scallop." Byssal threads, which help hold it in the sand, are woven into cloth for small garments in Mediterranean countries. Penshells are the only shellfish in North Carolina's marine waters known to produce a valuable pearl.

stiff penshell

• **stiff penshell** *Atrina rigida* (Lightfoot)
Description: (10 inches) Large, fragile, fan-shaped shell. Fewer than 20 ribs, some with large spines. One side straight and the other rounded. Resembles **half-naked penshell** except on mid-interior of shell, where large muscle scar borders the edge of nacreous area.
Color: Dark purplish black exterior. Pearly interior.
Habitat: Lives in sounds. Found on sound and ocean beaches after winter storms.
Range: North Carolina to Florida.
Notes: Also called a **rigid penshell**. See **sawtooth penshell** ***Notes***. See the photograph for an outline of the muscle scar and nacreous area on the left valve.

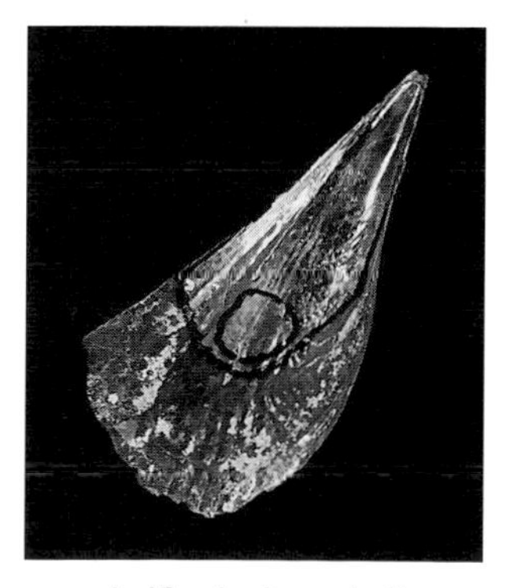
half-naked penshell

• **half-naked penshell** *Atrina seminuda* (Lamarck)
Description: (10 inches) Similar to **stiff penshell** except on mid-interior of shell. Large muscle scar surrounded by nacreous area, which extends to the narrow beak end of the shell. (On **stiff penshell**, large muscle scar on the edge of nacreous area.)
Color: Dark purplish black exterior. Pearly interior.
Habitat: Lives offshore in sandy mud. Occasionally found on ocean beaches after winter storms.
Range: North Carolina to Argentina.
Notes: See **sawtooth penshell** ***Notes***. See the photograph for an outline of the muscle scar and nacreous area.

CLAM-SHAPED – venus clams (Veneridae)

northern quahog (hard-shelled clam)

• northern quahog (hard-shelled clam) *Mercenaria mercenaria* (Linnaeus)

Description: (4 1/2 inches) Heavy, rounded, somewhat inflated shell. Concentric ridges on surface smooth near the center and stronger near the lower edge. Elevated beak. Strong lateral and cardinal teeth on hinge. Lunule and pallial sinus.
Color: Dull gray exterior, occasionally with purple zigzag markings. Dull gray interior, often with some dark purple near the pallial sinus.
Habitat: Lives in sounds and mouths of estuaries near the ocean. Commonly found on sound and ocean beaches.
Range: Canada to Texas.
Notes: Also known as the **littleneck clam**, **cherrystone** and **chowder clam**. A large commercial fishery in North Carolina waters, it has potential for mariculture. Nearly all individuals are male the first year, then about half become females. It was a favorite food of early Native Americans, who made beads from this shell's purple edge and used them as money, called "wampum." A form of this species with purple zigzag markings was once given the subspecies name *Mercenaria mercenaria notata* Say, but this clam is a naturally occurring genetic color form of the **northern quahog**. The purple zigzag pattern occurs in a number of other species in the family *Veneridae*. Specimens with these markings were once specifically bred by clam growers to identify their stock from nonhatchery-bred clams. Clams with these markings may still occasionally be found.

southern quahog

• southern quahog *Mercenaria campechiensis* (Gmelin)
Description: (6 inches) Heavy, rounded, inflated shell. Closely related to the **northern quahog** except surface sharply ridged in the central area. Many concentric ridges on surface. Strong lateral and cardinal teeth on hinge. Lunule and pallial sinus. Fine crenulations on bottom edge.
Color: Dull grayish white exterior. Interior usually all white but occasionally tinged with some purple.
Habitat: Lives offshore in fine sand near inlets at depths of 40 to 50 feet or more. Commonly found washed onto ocean beaches.
Range: Virginia to Texas.
Notes: A bed between Cape Lookout and Beaufort Inlet was fished commercially at one time. The **northern** and **southern quahogs** seem to hybridize in North Carolina inlets. Hybrid specimens may grow to 6 inches long.

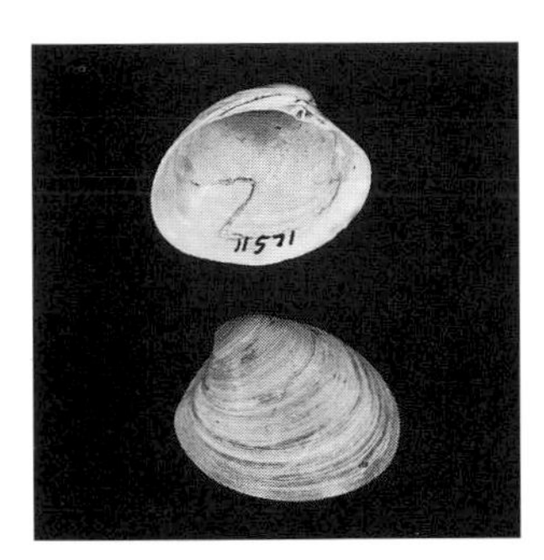

false quahog

• **false quahog** *Pitar morrhuanus* Linsley
Description: (1 1/2 inches) Looks like a small quahog but not as heavy. Smooth concentric lines on exterior. Bottom edge not crenulated. Lateral and cardinal teeth on hinge. Lunule and pallial sinus.
Color: Dull rusty-gray exterior. White interior.
Habitat: Commonly found on ocean beaches.
Range: Canada to North Carolina.
Notes: It is one of North Carolina's most common beach shells, but live specimens are rarely found.

calico clam

◊ • **calico clam** *Macrocallista maculata* (Linnaeus)
Description: (3 1/2 inches) Round to oval-shaped shell with smooth, shiny surface. Lateral and cardinal teeth on hinge. Lunule and large pallial sinus. Bottom edge not crenulated.
Color: Creamy exterior with purplish brown checkerboard pattern and usually one or two darker radiating bands. Polished white interior.
Habitat: Lives offshore at 50- to 120-foot depths south of Cape Lookout. The animal buries itself in the sand. Occasionally found on ocean beaches south of Cape Hatteras.
Range: North Carolina to Brazil.
Notes: Also called a **checkerboard clam** or **spotted venus**. This species tastes delicious.

sunray venus

• **sunray venus** *Macrocallista nimbosa* (Lightfoot)
Description: (7 1/2 inches) Large, smooth, glossy, elongate to triangular shell with rounded ends. Light concentric and radial lines. Lateral and cardinal teeth on hinge. Large lunule and small pallial sinus. No crenulations on bottom.
Color: Grayish salmon exterior, often with dull lavender, radial stripes (colors fade rapidly in the sun). Glossy whitish interior.
Habitat: Lives from intertidal zone of sounds to offshore depths greater than 65 feet. It buries itself just below the surface. Commonly found on sound and ocean beaches below Cape Hatteras (particularly Cape Lookout).
Range: North Carolina to Texas.
Notes: Fished commercially in Florida, this clam makes an excellent chowder.

cross-barred venus

• cross-barred venus *Chione cancellata* (Linnaeus)
Description: (1 3/4 inches) Rounded, triangular shell. Strong concentric ridges and strong radial ribbing form a raised crisscross pattern of ridges. Crenulations on bottom edge. Lateral and cardinal teeth on hinge. Lunule and small pallial sinus.
Color: Grayish yellow-white exterior. Occasionally has a few lavender radial stripes. Interior usually purple.
Habitat: Commonly lives on sandy bottoms of sounds and shallow offshore waters. Shells common on sound and ocean beaches.
Range: North Carolina to Brazil.
Notes: Although it is sweeter-tasting than the **northern quahog**, it is eaten only rarely.

lady-in-waiting venus

• lady-in-waiting venus *Chione intapurpurea* (Conrad)
Description: (1 1/2 inches) Round, thick shell. Many concentric ridges closer-set than those on the **cross-barred venus**. Serrated lower edges of concentric ridges give appearance of being crossed by light ribbing. Lateral and cardinal teeth on hinge. Lunule and pallial sinus. Fine crenulations on bottom edge of shell.
Color: Creamy white exterior, often with broken radial lavender stripes. White interior with purple markings.
Habitat: Lives offshore. Occasionally found on ocean beaches.
Range: North Carolina to Brazil.

imperial venus

• imperial venus *Chione latilirata* (Conrad)
Description: (1 1/2 inches) Rounded, triangular and well-inflated shell. Large, heavy concentric ridges rounded and often sharply shelved at the top. Ridges fragile on dry specimens. Bottom edge of ridges not serrated. Bottom edge of shell finely grooved. Cardinal and lateral teeth on hinge. Lunule and pallial sinus.
Color: Tan exterior with lavender blotches and radial stripes.
Habitat: Lives offshore, south of Cape Hatteras, in 60- to 120-foot depths. Occasionally found on ocean beaches.
Range: North Carolina to Brazil.
Notes: This species was frequently found among catches of the **Atlantic calico scallop** fishery.

gray pygmy-venus

• **gray pygmy-venus** *Chione grus* (Holmes)
Description: (3/8 inch) Oblong shell. Beak about one-quarter of the shell length from the rounded front end. Squarish back end. Surface with many fine radial ribs crossed by equally fine concentric lines. Lateral and cardinal teeth on hinge. Narrow, heart-shaped lunule. Small pallial sinus.
Color: Exterior gray to white (sometimes light pink) with purplish brown near both ends of the hinge. Dark brown lunule. White interior with purplish brown near one end.
Habitat: Lives in sand and mud in high-salinity estuaries south of Cape Hatteras and also in offshore waters up to 100 feet deep. Attaches to shells in shell-reef areas. Common on ocean beaches.
Range: North Carolina to Florida and Texas.

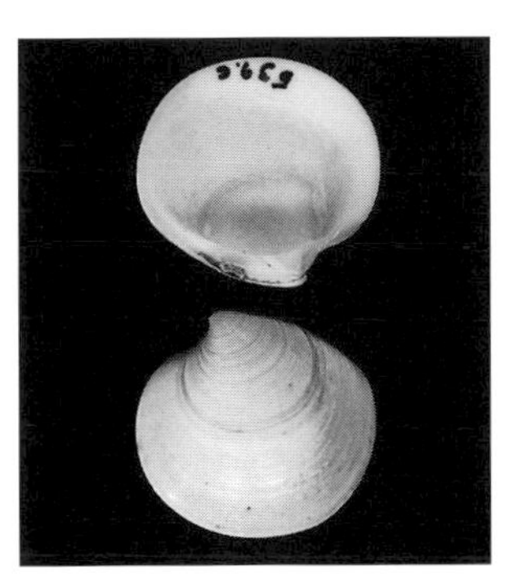

disk dosinia

• **disk dosinia** *Dosinia discus* (Reeve)
Description: (3 inches) Round, flat, disklike shell similar to **elegant dosinia**. Fine concentric ridges — about 50 ridges per inch. Beak curves forward. Cardinal teeth on hinge. Lunule and pallial sinus.
Color: Shiny white interior and exterior. Thin, yellow periostracum.
Habitat: Lives in sounds and just offshore on shallow sand flats. Commonly found on sound and ocean beaches.
Range: Virginia to Yucatan.

elegant dosinia

• **elegant dosinia** *Dosinia elegans* Conrad (= *Dosinia concentrica* Born)
Description: (4 inches) Round, flat, disklike shell. Similar to **disk dosinia** except for larger and less crowded concentric ridges — about 25 ridges per inch. Beak curves forward. Cardinal teeth on hinge. Lunule and pallial sinus.
Color: Pure white exterior and interior.
Habitat: Lives offshore in deeper waters than those reported for the **disk dosinia**. Often found on Cape Lookout ocean beaches.
Range: North Carolina to Brazil.
Notes: Empty shells found on beaches are often still attached at the hinge.

thin cyclinella

• **thin cyclinella** *Cyclinella tenuis* (Recluz)
Description: (1 1/4 inches) Round, moderately inflated shell. Resembles a small dosinia but lacks the closely spaced concentric ridges. Smooth surface with occasional concentric growth ridges. Small beak points forward noticeably. Thin-shelled. Faint lunule. Pallial sinus points toward beak.
Color: Dull white exterior and interior. If present, periostracum light gray.
Habitat: Lives in the soft bottoms of high-salinity estuaries. In North Carolina, collected mainly near Middle Marsh and at 30-foot depths off Atlantic Beach.
Range: Virginia to Florida, Texas and Brazil.
Notes: It is also called a **small ring clam** and **Atlantic cyclinella**.

CLAM-SHAPED – ocean quahogs (Arcticidae)

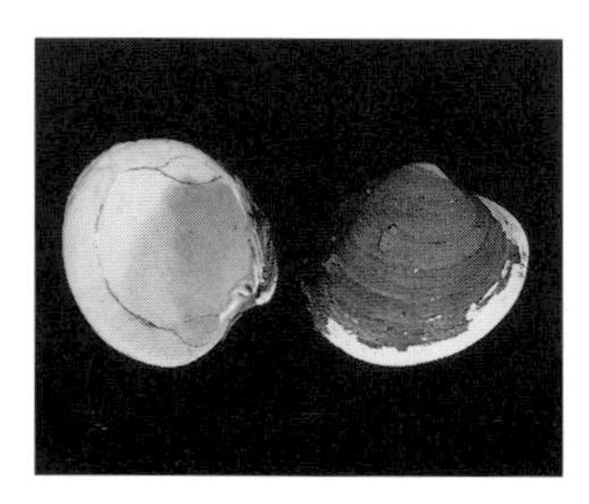

ocean quahog

• **ocean quahog** *Arctica islandica* (Linnaeus)
Description: (4 1/2 inches) Heavy shell similar in shape and size to the **northern quahog**, but has no lunule or pallial sinus. Fine crenulations on bottom edge. Periostracum coarse, shiny and wrinkled.
Color: Whitish exterior. White interior. Dark brown or black periostracum.
Habitat: Lives offshore in beds of sandy mud.
Range: Newfoundland, Canada, to Cape Hatteras, N.C.
Notes: It is also called a **mahogany clam** or **black clam**. A delicious species, it is not as popular as other clams, probably due to the orange color of its meat. It is fished commercially in New England.

CLAM-SHAPED – surfclams (Mactridae)

channeled duckclam

• **channeled duckclam** *Raeta plicatella* (Lamarck)
(= *Anatina plicatella, Labiosa canaliculata* Say)
Description: (2 3/4 inches) One end of oval shell narrow and pointed; other end broad and rounded. Strong concentric ridges. Thin-shelled. Lateral teeth not prominent. Ligament enclosed by triangular depression in hinge.
Color: Pure white exterior and interior.
Habitat: Lives in sand. Occasionally found on ocean beaches.
Range: North Carolina to Argentina.
Notes: It lives just below the surface of the sand and has two short, united siphons. The sexes are separate, and young are free-swimming.

smooth duckclam

• **smooth duckclam** *Anatina anatina* (Spengler)
(= *Labiosa lineata* Say)
Description: (2 3/4 inches) Similar to the **channeled duckclam** but more elongate with fine, rather than strong, concentric lines. Distinct rib on back slope of shell. Thin-shelled. Lateral teeth not prominent. Ligament enclosed by triangular depression.
Color: Cream-colored exterior and interior.
Habitat: Lives in shallow offshore waters. Not as common on ocean beaches as the **channeled duckclam**.
Range: North Carolina to Brazil.
Notes: It burrows just below the surface and has two short, united siphons. The sexes are separate, and young are free-swimming.

fragile surfclam

• **fragile surfclam** *Mactra fragilis* Gmelin
Description: (3 3/4 inches) Oval-shaped shell with broadly rounded ends. Smooth surface with many fine concentric lines. Thin shell with two radial ridges on its back slope. Central beak. Broad pallial sinus almost under beak. Lunule absent. Ligament enclosed by triangular depression in hinge. Lateral teeth present as strong, thin plates. Absence of fine transverse grooves on lateral teeth distinguishes small specimens from small **Atlantic surfclams**.
Color: White exterior and interior. Yellowish periostracum.
Habitat: Lives in sounds and shallow offshore waters. Occasionally found on sound and ocean beaches.
Range: North Carolina to Brazil.
Notes: See **channeled duckclam *Notes***.

Atlantic surfclam

• **Atlantic surfclam** *Spisula solidissima (*Dillwyn)
Description: (4 1/4 inches) Triangular shell with rounded ends. Smooth exterior with fine concentric lines. Triangular depression in hinge area just below the beak, which is almost central. Lateral teeth present as strong, thin plates with fine, inner transverse grooves. Narrow pallial sinus not extending under beak. No lunule.
Color: Yellowish or grayish white exterior. Dull white interior. Olive-brown periostracum.
Habitat: Lives offshore in beds north of Cape Hatteras. Frequently washed onto ocean beaches after storms.
Range: Nova Scotia, Canada, to South Carolina.
Notes: Also called the **beach clam**, **skimmer clam**, **hen clam** or **bar clam**, it is the largest common bivalve on North Carolina beaches (penshells are much larger but not common). Harvested along the New Jersey coast, it is the nation's largest molluscan fishery.

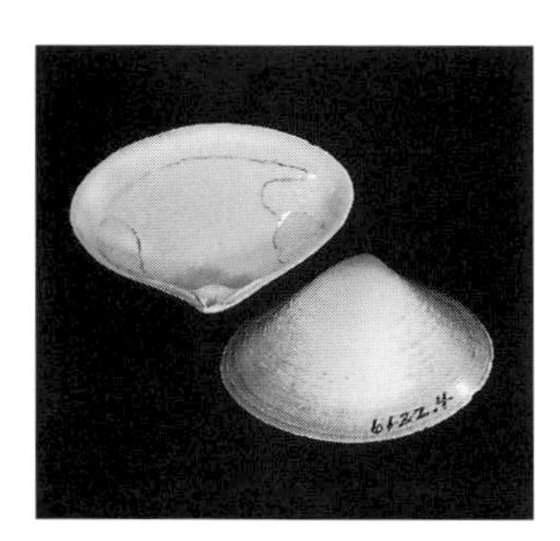

Ravenel surfclam

* • **Ravenel surfclam** *Spisula solidissima raveneli* Conrad
Description: (2 1/2 inches) Similar to **Atlantic surfclam** but shell lower in height and beak less bulbous.
Color: Similar to **Atlantic surfclam** except for lighter brown periostracum.
Habitat: Lives offshore in 10- to 30-foot depths. Commonly found near Cape Lookout and beaches south.
Range: North Carolina to Texas.
Notes: This species gradually replaces the **Atlantic surfclam** below the Virginia border. Specimens up to 4 or 5 inches long have been found north of Cape Lookout.

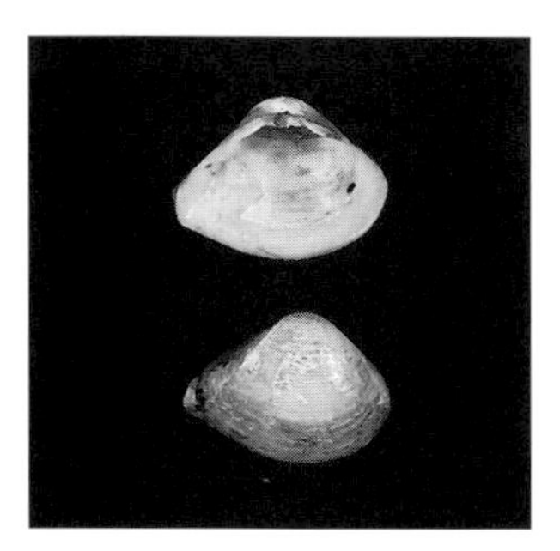

dwarf surfclam

• **dwarf surfclam** *Mulina lateralis* (Say)
Description: (3/4 inch) Small, rounded, thin shell. Resembles a small **Atlantic rangia** but lives in saltier estuaries. Smooth exterior with fine concentric lines; one radial ridge with tiny hairs runs down the more pointed end of the shell. Bulbous beak almost central and points forward. Small, spoon-shaped cavity in hinge area. Young of this species distinguished from young **Atlantic surfclams** by absence of fine inner transverse grooves on lateral hinge teeth.
Color: Light brown to ivory exterior. Whitish interior. Yellow periostracum.
Habitat: Common in estuaries with higher salinities than those containing **Atlantic rangia**. Common on sound and ocean beaches.
Range: Maine to Texas.
Notes: Also called a **duckclam**. Many marine fish and ducks depend on this clam for food. It lives just below the surface and has two short, united siphons. Young are free-swimming, and sexes are separate.

Atlantic rangia

• **Atlantic rangia** *Rangia cuneata* (Sowerby)
Description: (3 1/4 inches) Thick, rounded, triangular shell shaped somewhat like a quahog. Triangular cavity in hinge area. One end rounded and the other bluntly pointed and sloping. Frequently, periostracum attached. Young of this species distinguished from **dwarf surfclam** by absence of hairy ridge along the back slope of the shell.
Color: Grayish white exterior. Shiny white interior. Dark gray-brown periostracum.
Habitat: Lives commonly in low-salinity to almost freshwater areas of Albemarle and Croatan sounds and the Neuse and Pamlico rivers. Sometimes found living in large beds. Common on low-salinity sound beaches.
Range: Virginia to Texas.

Continued on upper right

Continued from lower left

Notes: Also called a **wedge rangia**, this species may be confused with the **Carolina marshclam. Atlantic rangia** has a heavier shell and a polished interior (see other differences in ***Description*** and ***Habitat***). A small commercial rangia fishery existed a few years ago. With the development of certain advances in food technology, this clam could become one of North Carolina's fishery resources.

CLAM-SHAPED – marshclams (Corbiculidae)

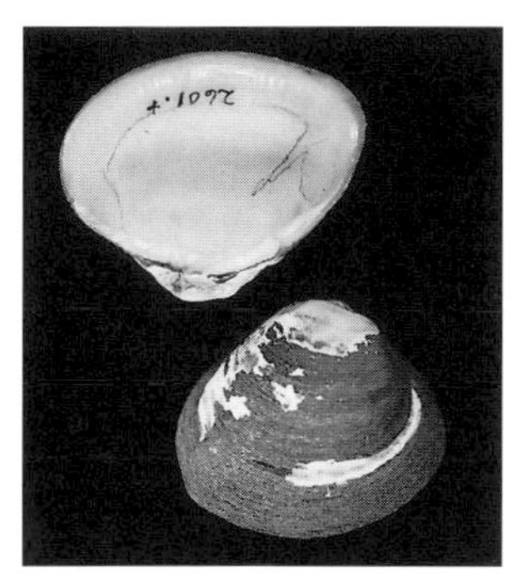

Carolina marshclam

• **Carolina marshclam** *Polymesoda caroliniana* (Bosc)
Description: (3 1/4 inches) Oval to rounded shell with concentric lines. Corroded areas common on exterior. Distinguished from **Atlantic rangia** by darker periostracum and lack of triangular or spoon-shaped cavity in the hinge.
Color: Light olive-brown exterior. Interior white but not polished. Dark brown periostracum.
Habitat: Lives in the mud of low-salinity marshes (areas more marshy than those where the **Atlantic rangia** lives).
Range: North Carolina to Texas.
Notes: The acids in brackish marshes cause the shell's surface to corrode.

CLAM-SHAPED – corbulas (Corbulidae)

contracted corbula

• **contracted corbula** *Corbula contracta* Say

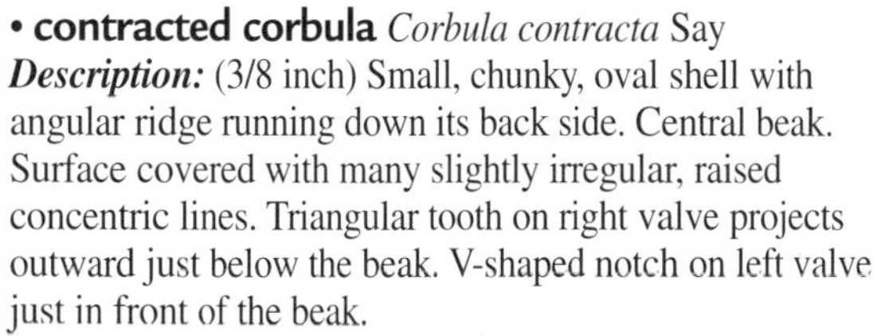

Description: (3/8 inch) Small, chunky, oval shell with angular ridge running down its back side. Central beak. Surface covered with many slightly irregular, raised concentric lines. Triangular tooth on right valve projects outward just below the beak. V-shaped notch on left valve just in front of the beak.
Color: Gray exterior. Whitish interior.
Habitat: Lives offshore in sand or mud at depths up to 100 feet. Occasionally lives in high-salinity estuaries. Commonly found on ocean beaches.
Range: Cape Cod, Mass., to Florida and Brazil.
Notes: This species is often found in the stomach of the sea star, *Astropecten articulatus*. Corbulas are difficult to identify because of their variable shapes.

Dietz corbula

• **Dietz corbula** *Corbula dietziana* C.B. Adams
Description: (1/2 inch) Similar to **contracted corbula** except (1) heavier and thicker shell, (2) coarser concentric ridges with microscopic threads between them and (3) very angular back ridge and back end.
Color: Gray to pinkish exterior. Pink rays often on bottom edges.
Habitat: Lives offshore in sand to depths of about 100 feet. Commonly on ocean beaches.
Range: North Carolina to Florida and Brazil.
Notes: This species is occasionally found in the stomach of the sea star, *Astropecten articulatus*. It has two growth phases. The first is that of a typical bivalve, with both valves growing at the same rate. In the second phase, the right valve grows nearly three times as much as the left valve. This change in growth produces part of the shell that is thicker and more angular than it was in the earlier phase.

CLAM-SHAPED – soft-shell clams (Myidae)

soft-shell

• **soft-shell** *Mya arenaria* Linnaeus
Description: (3 1/2 inches) Elliptical shell with fine concentric lines. Left valve has spoon-shaped cavity on a horizontal shelf that projects from the hinge area. Beak near center. Deep pallial sinus.
Color: White to gray exterior. White interior. Grayish brown periostracum.
Habitat: Lives in sounds and inlets with small specimens found south of Cape Hatteras. Large fossil shells frequently found on ocean beaches. Lives buried in mud and has long siphons. Adaptations allow it to survive exposure to air twice a day in the intertidal zone.
Range: Labrador, Canada, to South Carolina.
Notes: Also known as the **steamer clam**, it is a major fishery in some Northern states. Its delicious meat is the source of the famous Howard Johnson fried clams.

subovate soft-shell

• **subovate soft-shell** *Paramya subovata* (Conrad)
Description: (3/8 inch) Small, rectangular shell with rough concentric lines on surface. Beak slightly swollen and just off-center. Triangular depression on hinge with a raised tooth on either side. The major identifying mark: noticeable extension of the triangular depression into the shell cavity.
Color: Gray.
Habitat: Lives offshore at depths up to 75 feet. Commonly found on ocean beaches.

Continued on upper right

Continued from lower left

Range: Delaware to Florida and Texas.
Notes: This species has been reported to live beside the burrows of the marine worm *Thalassema hartmani.*

CLAM-SHAPED – crassinellas (Crassatellidae)

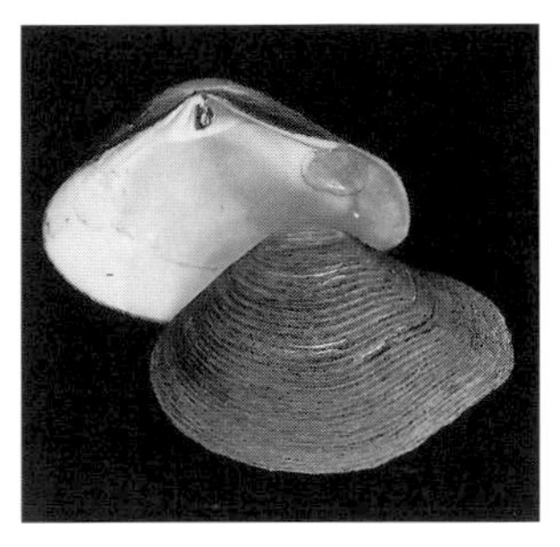

beautiful crassinella

lunate crassinella

• **beautiful crassinella** *Eucrassatella speciosa* (A. Adams)
Description: (2 1/2 inches) Thick shell with one end rounded and the other pulled out to form a blunt, hooklike extension. Closely spaced, heavy concentric ridges on surface. Beak near center. Two deep muscle scars on inside. No pallial sinus.
Color: Brown exterior. Interior usually pinkish.
Habitat: Lives offshore. Occasionally brought in by **calico scallop** fishers as incidental catch.
Range: North Carolina to West Indies.
Notes: Also called **Gibb's clam**.

• **lunate crassinella** *Crassinella lunulata* (Conrad)
Description: (1/4 inch) Small, solid, flat shell. Top edge straight but diverges from the beak at a sharp 90-degree angle. About 15 to 20 low, sharp, concentric ribs on surface.
Color: Cream to pink exterior, sometimes with brownish rays. Interior mostly brown.
Habitat: Lives offshore at depths greater than 100 feet. Commonly found on ocean beaches.
Range: Massachusetts to Florida, Texas and Brazil.

CLAM-SHAPED – semeles (Semelidae)

cancellate semele

• **cancellate semele** *Semele bellastriata* (Conrad)
Description: (1 inch) Small, oval, narrow shell. Radial and concentric ribbing on exterior, creating a beaded look. Beak subcentral. Hinge teeth. Ligament embedded in spoon-shaped cavity in hinge area. Pallial sinus deep and rounded. Narrow lunule.
Color: Cream exterior with pinkish purple specks or blotches. Occasionally solid purplish gray. Shiny interior, often bright yellow or lavender.
Habitat: Lives offshore in sand and mud and has long siphons. Known at depths up to 300 feet. Occasionally found on ocean beaches south of Cape Hatteras.
Range: North Carolina to Florida, Texas and Brazil.
Notes: This species tastes good but isn't abundant enough to be commercially valuable.

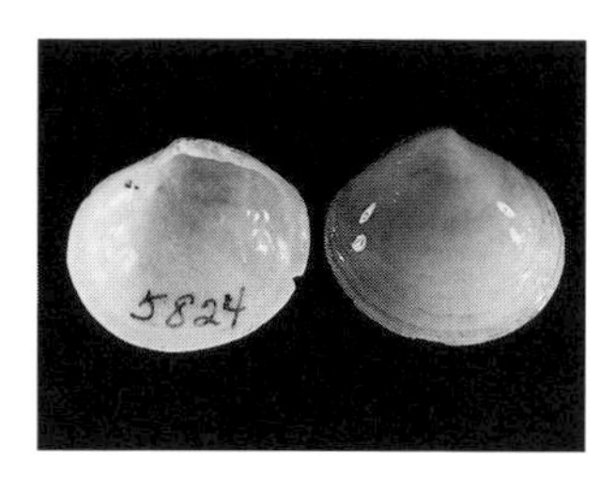

Atlantic semele

• **Atlantic semele** *Semele proficua* (Pulteney)
Description: (1 1/2 inches) Broadly oval to almost round shell. Fine, sharp concentric lines 1/16 inch apart. Central beak points forward. Small lunule. Lateral teeth on hinge and a narrow spoon-shaped cavity. Pallial sinus deep and rounded.
Color: Creamy white exterior, sometimes with pinkish red rays. Shiny white interior, sometimes yellowish with light reddish speckles.
Habitat: Lives in sounds and shallow offshore waters. Sometimes washed onto sound and ocean beaches.
Range: North Carolina to Argentina.
Notes: Also called a **white Atlantic semele**. See **cancellate semele *Notes***.

tellin semele

• **tellin semele** *Cumingia tellinoides* (Conrad)
Description: (1 inch) Small, thin, oval shell with one end rounded and the other almost pointed. Many fine concentric ridges. Central beak. Spoon-shaped cavity in hinge area. Rounded pallial sinus.
Color: White exterior and interior.
Habitat: Lives in sounds and shallow offshore water attached to driftwood and shells. Occasionally found on ocean beaches.
Range: Nova Scotia, Canada, to Florida.
Notes: Also called a **common cumingia**. See **cancellate semele *Notes***.

Atlantic abra

• **Atlantic abra** *Abra aequalis* (Say)
Description: (1/2 inch) Smooth, plump, almost circular shell. Beak area somewhat angular. Fine concentric ribbing near the edge of shell. Front edge of shell grooved. Thin-shelled. Hinge teeth. Large, rounded pallial sinus.
Color: Exterior white and slightly iridescent. Whitish interior.
Habitat: Lives commonly in sounds, mouths of estuaries and shallow offshore waters. Common on sound and ocean beaches.
Range: North Carolina to Brazil.
Notes: See **cancellate semele *Notes***.

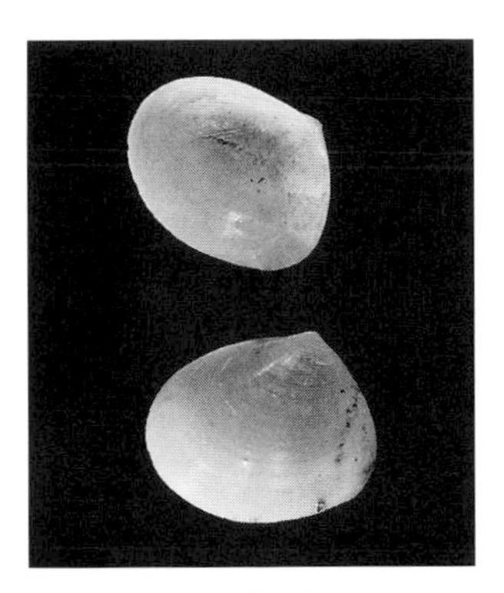

smooth abra

• **smooth abra** *Abra lioica* (Dall)
Description: (3/8 inch) Similar to the **Atlantic abra** except (1) shape more elongate, (2) beak more forward and pronounced and (3) front edge of right valve not grooved.
Color: See **Atlantic abra.**
Habitat: Lives in high-salinity estuaries and offshore to depths of about 100 feet. Occasionally found on ocean beaches.
Range: Cape Cod, Mass., to Florida and West Indies.

CLAM-SHAPED – lucines (Lucinidae)

cross-hatched lucine

• **cross-hatched lucine** *Divaricalla quadrisulcata* (d'Orbigny)
Description: (3/4 inch) Small, rounded, plump shell. Pattern of tiny grooves swirl around surface, resulting in a chevronlike sculpture. Hinge teeth. Crenulations on inside edges. No pallial sinus.
Color: White.
Habitat: Lives in shallow to offshore water. Common on ocean beaches.
Range: Massachusetts to Brazil.
Notes: Shells are often used in crafts.

buttercup lucine

• **buttercup lucine** *Anodontia alba* Link
Description: (2 3/4 inches) Rounded, plump shell. Smooth exterior except for fine concentric sculpture. Indistinct hinge teeth. Long muscle scar on inside. No pallial sinus.
Color: Dull white exterior with bright yellowish orange on the sides. Interior tinged with yellow to orange.
Habitat: Lives in shallow to offshore waters. Occasionally washed onto ocean beaches.
Range: North Carolina to West Indies.
Notes: See **cross-hatched lucine** *Notes*.

many-line lucine

• **many-line lucine** *Parvilucina multilineata* (Tuomey & Holmes)
Description: (3/8 inch) Small, circular, robust shell with low ridge from the prominent beak to the back bottom edge of the shell. Sculptured surface with many incised concentric lines crossed by many finely incised radial lines. Cardinal and lateral teeth on hinge. Small and smooth lunule. Bottom edge of shell crenulated. No pallial sinus.
Color: White.
Habitat: Lives in moderate- to high-salinity estuaries and offshore (common in 50-foot depths and occasionally in 100-foot depths). Commonly washed onto ocean beaches.
Range: Virginia to Florida and Brazil.
Notes: This species is often found in the stomach of the sea star, *Astropecten articulatus*.

Pennsylvania lucine

• **Pennsylvania lucine** *Linga pensylvanica* (Linnaeus)
Description: (2 1/2 inches) Round, thick shell with delicate to strong concentric ridges on outer surface. Pronounced furrow from beak to back bottom edge of the shell. Well-marked lunule with a raised center. Cardinal and lateral hinge teeth present. No pallial sinus but well-marked pallial line. On recently living specimens, the thin periostracum may be ridged concentrically outward and flaked off easily.
Color: White exterior and interior. Yellow periostracum.
Habitat: Known living in sand offshore of Core Banks and Cape Fear. Rarely found on ocean beaches.
Range: North Carolina to Florida and Brazil.
Notes: The large size allows it to wash ashore occasionally.

dosinia lucine

• **dosinia lucine** *Lucinia keenae* Chavan (= *L. radians* Conrad)
Description: (3/4 inch) Disklike shell with many fine concentric ridges on the surface. Ridges cut by finer radial lines, especially near the beak and front edge. Moderately high beak points over a submerged lunule. Inside edge often lightly crenulated. Weak lateral and strong cardinal teeth on hinge. No pallial sinus.
Color: White.
Habitat: Known living from 50- to 100-foot depths offshore of Beaufort Inlet. Collected by divers from 40 feet.
Range: North Carolina to Florida and West Indies.

woven lucine

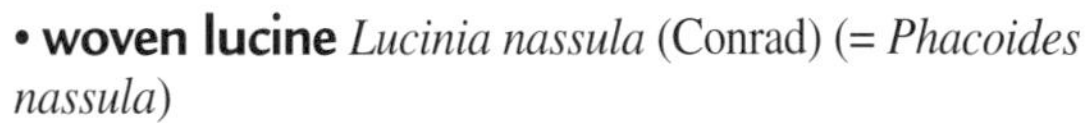

• **woven lucine** *Lucinia nassula* (Conrad) (= *Phacoides nassula*)
Description: (1/2 inch) Moderately compressed, disklike shell. Rough, reticulated surface often with raised scales at the juncture of concentric and radial lines. Moderately high beak with small pit in front. Strong lateral and cardinal teeth on hinge. No pallial sinus. Strongly crenulated inside edge.
Color: White.
Habitat: Known living off Beaufort Inlet at depths from 30 to 100 feet. Occasionally washed onto ocean beaches.
Range: North Carolina to Florida, Texas and Bahamas.

CLAM-SHAPED – diplodons (Ungulinidae)

Atlantic diplodon

• **Atlantic diplodon** *Diplodonta punctata* (Say)
Description: (1/2 inch or more) Strongly inflated, round shell. Smooth surface incised with fine concentric growth lines. Thin-shelled. Two cardinal teeth on hinge of each valve, one of them split. No lateral teeth on hinge.
Color: White.
Habitat: Lives offshore in sand at depths of 50 feet or more. Occasionally washed onto ocean beaches.
Range: North Carolina to Florida and Brazil.
Notes: Note the drill hole made by moonsnails in the photo.

CLAM-SHAPED – tellins (Tellinidae)

Balthic macoma

• **Balthic macoma** *Macoma balthica* (Linnaeus)
Description: (1 inch) Small, oval to round, almost wedge-shaped shell. Many fine concentric lines. Central beak not bulbous. Thin-shelled. Hinge with cardinal teeth only.
Color: Dull pinkish white exterior. Shiny white interior. Olive-brown periostracum on bottom portion of shell.
Habitat: Lives commonly on mud bottoms in low-salinity areas, such as coastal creeks, rivers and sounds. Occasionally found on sound beaches.
Range: Arctic Sea to Georgia.
Notes: A deposit feeder, it burrows into mud and has a long incurrent siphon and a short excurrent siphon.

Mitchell macoma

• **Mitchell macoma** *Macoma mitchelli* Dall
(= *M. phenax* Dall)
Description: (3/4 inch) Somewhat oblong, almost wedge-shaped shell. Lower edge almost flat and not as rounded as the **Balthic macoma**. Concentric growth lines. Beak not quite central and not bulbous. Hinge with cardinal teeth only.
Color: Dull white exterior.
Habitat: Lives in estuaries with higher salinities than those containing the **Atlantic rangia.** Less common in estuarine rivers and sounds than the **Balthic macoma**. Occasionally found on sound beaches.
Range: Virginia to Texas.
Notes: See **Balthic macoma** ***Notes***.

elongate macoma

• **elongate macoma** *Macoma tenta* (Say)
Description: (3/4 inch) Elliptical, elongate shell with a smooth surface. Beak slightly back from center. Back end of shell slightly twisted and narrower than the anterior end. No lateral teeth on hinge, but two narrow cardinal teeth on right valve and one cardinal tooth on left valve. Large pallial sinus.
Color: Iridescent white exterior. Gray periostracum.
Habitat: Lives primarily in moderate- to high-salinity estuaries. Occasionally found offshore to depths of about 100 feet. Sometimes found on sound and ocean beaches.
Range: Prince Edward Island, Canada, to Florida and Brazil.
Notes: Also called a **narrowed macoma** or **tenta macoma**.

white strigilla

• **white strigilla** *Strigilla mirabilis* (Philippi)
Description: (3/8 inch) Small, rounded, moderately inflated shell with off-center beak. Easily recognized by the strongly cut oblique lines on the surface. Large pallial sinus but difficult to see. Inner edge not crenulated.
Color: Shiny white.
Habitat: Known to live offshore at depths of 10 feet to more than 100 feet off Beaufort Inlet and south. Occasionally washed onto ocean beaches south of Cape Hatteras.
Range: North Carolina to Texas and Brazil.
Notes: Also called **remarkable scraper**.

alternate tellin

• alternate tellin *Tellina alternata* Say
Description: (2 1/2 inches) Solid, elliptical shell (longer than high, not very wide). Subcentral beak. Many concentric lines, fine but prominent. Shell round in front and angular in back.
Color: Shiny white exterior, sometimes pinkish or yellowish. White interior. Yellowish periostracum.
Habitat: Lives in shallow and offshore waters. Frequently washed onto ocean beaches.
Range: North Carolina to Brazil.
Notes: Also called a **lined tellin**. It feeds on bottom detritus, burrows deep into the sand and has a long siphon. About 16 tellins are known in North Carolina off the coast and in the estuaries. All are much smaller than the **alternate tellin** except the **great-tellin**, which may reach 5 inches long.

shiny dwarf-tellin

◊ **• shiny dwarf-tellin** *Tellina nitens* C.B. Adams (= *T. georgeana* Dall)
Description: (1 1/2 inches) Almost identical in shape and sculpture to **alternate tellin** but smaller with weaker growth lines and different color.
Color: Reddish orange.
Habitat: Lives offshore. Frequently brought up from the **Atlantic calico scallop** beds.
Range: North Carolina to Texas and Brazil.

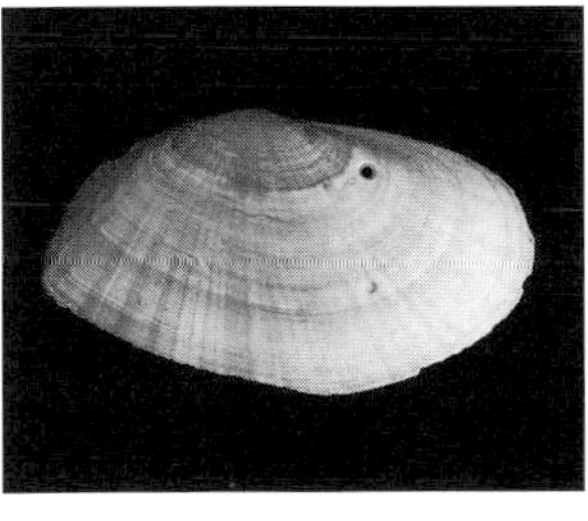

great-tellin

◊ **• great-tellin** *Tellina magna* Spengler
Description: (5 inches) Large shell. Both ends slope to rounded margin with back end more pointed. Strong hinge with cardinal and lateral teeth. Smooth surface marked by growth lines. Pallial sinus.
Color: Exterior of left valve white; exterior of right valve yellowish or orange. Interior often pinkish.
Habitat: Lives in estuaries and offshore.
Range: North Carolina to West Indies.
Notes: Rare. Sought by collectors.

northern dwarf-tellin

• **northern dwarf-tellin** *Tellina agilis* Stimpson
Description: (1/2 inch, but usually smaller) Small, elliptical shell with a rounded front end and a shorter, sloping back end. Beak behind the center. Smooth surface with microscopic, concentric threads that are strongest over the back shoulder area. Large pallial sinus almost touching front muscle scar. Right valve hinge with one lateral and one cardinal tooth; left valve hinge with one cardinal but no lateral tooth.
Color: Front of exterior shiny to iridescent creamy white, occasionally with pinkish tints. Interior white.
Habitat: Lives in mud flats of moderate- to high-salinity estuaries. Less commonly lives offshore to depths of 75 feet or more. Common on ocean beaches.
Range: Gulf of St. Lawrence, Canada, to Georgia.

many-colored tellin

• **many-colored tellin** *Tellina versicolor* DeKay
Description: (1/2 inch) Similar to **northern dwarf-tellin** except more elongate with a steeply sloping back edge and a flat bottom edge. Strongly incised concentric lines on surface spaced widely and evenly. These lines strong on the back slope of the right valve. Typical *Tellina* teeth on hinge. Pallial sinus close to the front muscle scar and partly attached to it.
Color: Exterior shiny, iridescent white to red, frequently marked with radial rays of white to red.
Habitat: Lives offshore in sand to about 100-foot depths and occasionally in high-salinity estuaries. Occasionally washed onto ocean beaches.
Range: Rhode Island to Florida, Texas and West Indies.
Notes: Also called **DeKay's dwarf-tellin**.

rainbow tellin

• **rainbow tellin** *Tellina iris* Say
Description: (1/2 inch) Small shell, shaped similarly to the **many-colored tellin** but distinguished by surface sculpture. On this shell, concentric lines cut angularly by microscopic lines (appropriately called sissulations), whereas no sissulations on the **many-colored tellin**.
Color: White to red (or may be rayed with white or red).
Habitat: Lives in high-salinity estuaries and offshore to depths of about 50 feet or more. Occasionally found on ocean beaches.
Range: North Carolina to Florida and Texas.
Notes: Also called an **iris tellin**.

sybaritic tellin

• **sybaritic tellin** *Tellina sybaritica* Dall
Description: (3/8 inch) Small, elongate, tellin-shaped shell somewhat thickened and not compressed. Front of top edge long and slightly convex; back of top edge short and slightly concave. Bottom edge convex. Closely spaced, strongly incised lines on surface. Typical *Tellina* teeth on hinge. Pallial sinus approaches front muscle scar but then turns down to merge with the pallial line.
Color: Exterior white to watermelon-red.
Habitat: Lives offshore in sand south of Cape Hatteras from depths of 30 to 100 feet or more. Occasionally washed onto ocean beaches.
Range: North Carolina to Florida and Brazil.
Notes: Also called **Dall's dwarf-tellin.**

slandered tellin

• **slandered tellin** *Tellina probrina* Boss
Description: (3/8 inch) Elongated oval to almost rectangular, compressed shell. Fragile. Weak, irregularly spaced, concentrically incised lines on surface. No radial lines. Front edge of shell concave; back edge broadly rounded with a flat, oblique truncation. Typical *Tellina* teeth on hinge. Pallial sinus well separated from the front adductor muscle scar.
Color: Shiny white exterior. Periostracum may make the surface iridescent.
Habitat: Lives offshore south of Cape Hatteras from depths of 30 to 60 feet or more. Occasionally washed onto ocean beaches.
Range: North Carolina to Florida and Texas.
Notes: Also called **Boss' dwarf-tellin.**

striate tellin

• **striate tellin** *Tellina aequistriata* Say
Description: (1 inch) Oval, compressed shell. Beak back of center and higher than in most *Tellina* species (about three-quarters of total shell length). Surface covered with raised, thin concentric ribbing that is strongest toward the back end. Back edge a straight line, but two radial ridges on the right valve and one radial ridge on the left valve make the back end appear slightly pointed. Both lateral and cardinal teeth on hinge. Pallial sinus does not touch front muscle scar.
Color: White.
Habitat: Lives in mud flats south of Cape Hatteras, in high-salinity estuaries and offshore to depths of about 100 feet or more. Most common in offshore depths between 10 and 50 feet. Occasionally washed onto sound and ocean beaches.
Range: North Carolina to Texas and Brazil.

CLAM-SHAPED – coquinas (Donacidae)

variable coquina

• **variable coquina** *Donax variabilis* Say (= *D. roemeri protracta* Conrad)
Description: (1 inch) Small, elongate, triangular shell. Smooth exterior with ribbing at beak end of shell. Hinge teeth.
Color: Extremely variable coloration — white, yellow, orange, pink, red and purple in solids, ringed or rayed patterns.
Habitat: Lives in the intertidal zone of sandy ocean beaches.
Range: New York to Texas.
Notes: Also called a **Florida coquina**, **butterfly shell**, **wedge shell** or **pompano**. Often seen along the tide line of sandy beaches, where waves continually uncover these shallowly buried clams and wash them farther up the beach. Each time the coquina is exposed, its small, muscular foot immediately emerges and stands the animal on end as it burrows down an inch or two into the wet sand. Coquinas can survive in dry sand for up to three days. They make a delicious broth.

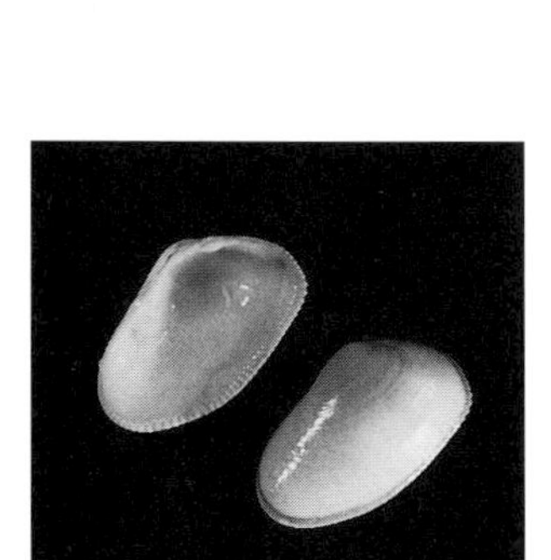

parvula coquina

* • **parvula coquina** *Donax parvula* Philippi
Description: (1/2 inch) Resembles the **variable coquina** except slightly elliptical and less triangular with a smoother and more rounded beak end.
Color: Similar to that of the **variable coquina**.
Habitat: Near and just below the low tide line of ocean inlet beaches (lower on the beach than the **variable coquina**).
Range: South of Cape Lookout, N.C., to Florida.
Notes: Populations of this shell are known at the mouth of the Newport River at Fort Macon State Park. It should also be found at similar inlet locations farther south.

CLAM-SHAPED – wedgeclams (Mesodesmatidae)

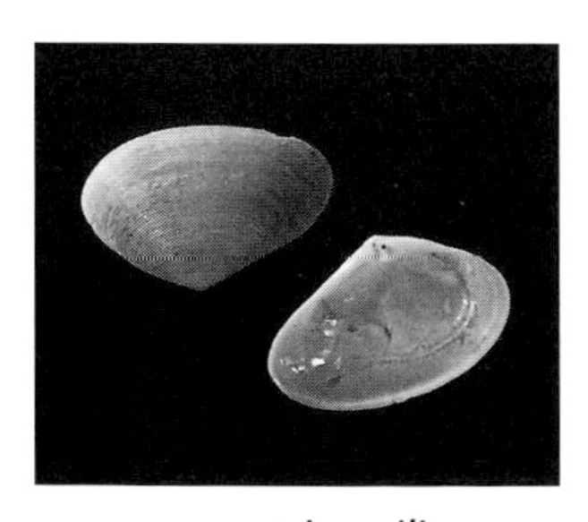

concentric ervilia

• **concentric ervilia** *Ervilia concentrica* (Holmes)
Description: (1/4 inch) Oval shell with a slightly off-center beak. Many fine concentric ridges on surface. Triangular ligament pit on hinge and a prominent cardinal tooth on both valves. Large pallial sinus.
Color: Cream exterior. Shiny and translucent interior.
Habitat: Lives offshore at 30- to 100-foot depths. Also has been found in the estuarine waters of Bogue Sound. Occasionally to commonly washed onto ocean beaches.
Range: North Carolina to Florida and Brazil.

CLAM-SHAPED – spoonclams (Periplomatidae)

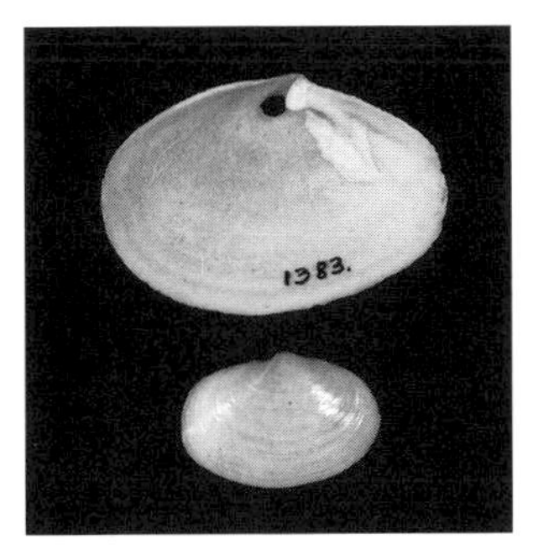

Lea spoonclam

• **Lea spoonclam** *Periploma leanum* (Conrad)
Description: (1 3/4 inches) Oval shell with one end slightly squared off. Left valve less convex than right valve. Spoon-shaped cavity in hinge area of both valves, beginning as a narrow slit in the beak and extending into the shell cavity. Blunt end of shell has internal rib or crease running from hinge cavity to about halfway down the lower edge. Fine, raised rib running parallel to crease reinforces the spoon-shaped cavity. No cardinal or lateral teeth on hinge. Small pallial sinus.
Color: White exterior and interior. Yellow periostracum.
Habitat: Lives just offshore. Not commonly washed onto ocean beaches.
Range: Nova Scotia, Canada, to North Carolina.

CLAM-SHAPED – pandoras (Pandoridae)

threeline pandora

• **threeline pandora** *Pandora trilineata* Say
Description: (1 inch) Small, crescent-shaped, flat shell with one end shaped like a small tube. Concave upper edge. Rough concentric growth lines on surface. Strong cardinal teeth radiating from beak. Worn shells with pearly layer below. No pallial sinus.
Color: White exterior. Pearly interior.
Habitat: Lives buried just below the surface in sounds and shallow offshore areas. Rarely seen on beaches by collectors.
Range: Virginia to Texas.
Notes: Also called **Say's pandora**. It is one of five similar species found in this habitat. Animal has short, united siphons.

CLAM-SHAPED – lyonsias (Lyonsiidae)

glassy lyonsia

• **glassy lyonsia** *Lyonsia hyalina* Conrad
Description: (3/4 inch) Small, very fragile shell with rounded ends. Beak not central but located about one-third of the way in from shell's end. Fine radial ribbing on surface. No teeth on hinge. Sand grains often stuck to the periostracum.
Color: Pearly grayish white exterior. White interior. Yellowish brown periostracum.
Habitat: Lives in estuaries and offshore.
Range: Canada to South Carolina.
Notes: A closely related species, the **pearly entodesma** or

Continued on next page

Continued from previous page

pearly lyonsia, *Entodesma beana* (d'Orbigny), is occasionally found offshore in sponges. It may be gathered by scuba divers in the Cape Fear area. This species is generally larger and more swollen at its anterior end than the **glassy lyonsia**.

CLAM-SHAPED – geoducks (Hiatellidae)

Atlantic geoduck

• **Atlantic geoduck** *Panopea bitruncata* Conrad
Description: (8 1/4 inches) Large, almost rectangular shell with a rounded front end and a blunt, concave back end. Rough concentric ridges on surface but smooth bottom edge. Teeth on hinge. Short but indented pallial sinus.
Color: White to cream exterior and interior.
Habitat: Lives in shallow to offshore waters in burrows up to 4 feet deep. Bed of empty shells known off of Atlantic Beach near an artificial reef of sunken ships. Occasionally found on ocean beaches.
Range: North Carolina to Texas.
Notes: The closely related **Pacific geoduck**, *Panopea abrupta* (Conrad), from Puget Sound is reportedly one of the finest-tasting clams found along the West Coast.

ANGELWING-SHAPED – angelwings (Pholadidae)

angelwing

• **angelwing** *Cyrtopleura costata* (Linnaeus)
Description: (5 3/4 inches) Fairly large, elongate shell tapers to a rounded point. Strongly resembles the wing of an angel. About 30 sharply beaded ribs. Shell rolls outward on top — this edge not braced by partitions. Very thin shell breaks easily.
Color: Pure white exterior and interior, occasionally pink at the edges. Grayish periostracum.
Habitat: Lives offshore and in estuaries, burrowed as much as 3 feet deep in mud or clay. Occasionally washed onto beaches.
Range: New Jersey to Brazil.
Notes: This is a popular shell with delicious meat. The pink tinges occur when the animal feeds on a certain type of algae. It moves up and down in its burrows. If dug up, the fragile shell must be placed immediately into a container of water or it will close suddenly and shatter.

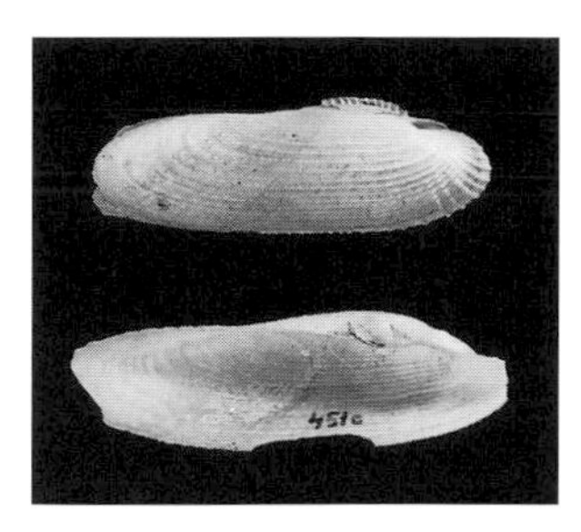
Campeche angelwing

• **Campeche angelwing** *Pholas campechiensis* Gmelin
Description: (3 3/4 inches) Resembles the **angelwing** except it is smaller, with weaker ribbing and numerous braces supporting the rolled-back hinge on its top surface.
Color: White exterior and interior.
Habitat: Lives offshore, burrowed deeply in stiff mud. Occasionally washed onto ocean beaches near and south of Cape Fear.
Range: North Carolina to Uruguay.
Notes: Live specimens rarely are found.

Atlantic mud-piddock

• **Atlantic mud-piddock** *Barnea truncata* (Say)
Description: (2 1/4 inches) Similar to **angelwing** but with weaker sculpture. One end squared off and other end pointed. Loose accessory plates above the hinge on live specimens.
Color: White exterior and interior.
Habitat: Lives burrowed into mud, clay or softwood. Occasionally washed onto sounds and ocean beaches.
Range: Maine to Brazil.
Notes: Also called a **fallen angelwing**. This fragile shell is rarely dug from mud without breaking. It burrows deeply and has long, united siphons.

wedge piddock

• **wedge piddock** *Martesia cuneiformis* (Say)
Description: (1/2 inch) Tiny, wedge-shaped shell with concentric ridges. Exterior groove runs from beak to bottom edge of each valve. Hinge line topped with a series of loose accessory plates.
Color: Whitish exterior, usually with brown stains. Whitish interior.
Habitat: Lives burrowed in submerged driftwood.
Range: North Carolina to Brazil.
Notes: Also called a **wedge-shaped martesia**. It is one of about six small boring clams found in North Carolina waters. Species are distinguished mainly by characteristics of their accessory plates. It destroys many wooden structures along the coast.

ANGELWING-SHAPED – rupellarias (Petricolidae)

false angelwing

• **false angelwing** *Petricola pholadiformis* Lamarck
Description: (2 3/4 inches) Thin, elongate shell resembling a small angelwing but lacks the rolled-out hinge area. Beak at one end of shell. Strong radial ribbing on the beak end. Teeth on hinge. Deep pallial sinus.
Color: White exterior and interior.
Habitat: Lives in intertidal zone, burrowed into hard clay or peat. Commonly found on sounds and ocean beaches.
Range: Canada to Uruguay.
Notes: It burrows into hard surfaces and has long, partially united siphons.

Atlantic rupellaria

• **Atlantic rupellaria** *Rupellaria typica* (Jonas)
(= *Petricola typica*)
Description: (1 inch) Variable shape, usually oblong. Coarse radial ribs. Beak about one-quarter of length from front end. Deep pallial sinus. No good lateral teeth.
Color: Grayish white exterior and brownish interior.
Habitat: Lives offshore in rock, shell or coral.
Range: North Carolina to Brazil.
Notes: Shell shape varies because it does not bore its own hole. Instead, it occupies crevices or holes bored by other animals and adopts the shape of the crevice or hole.

RAZOR-SHAPED – tagelus (Solecurtidae)

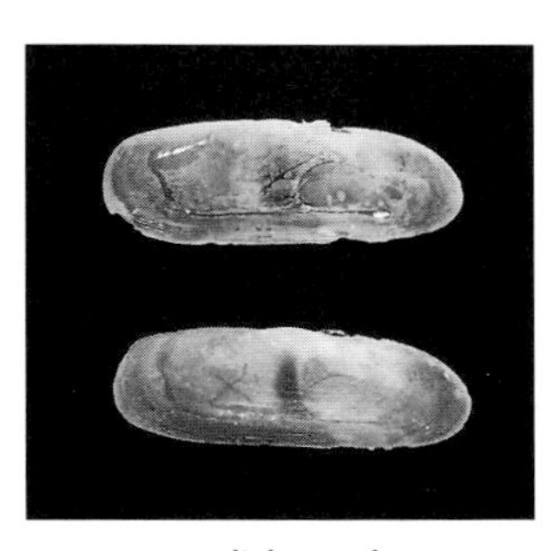

purplish tagelus

• **purplish tagelus** *Tagelus divisus* (Spengler)
Description: (1 1/4 inches) Fragile, rectangular shell with rounded ends. Smooth surface with concentric growth lines not overlain by oblique lines. Beak almost central. Small hinge teeth. Purplish raised rib in interior running from the beak to the lower shell edge. Large pallial sinus.
Color: Pale purplish gray exterior, often with a faint reddish brown streak near the edge. Purplish interior. Yellowish to greenish brown periostracum.
Habitat: Lives in sounds and offshore. Commonly found washed onto sounds and ocean beaches.
Range: Massachusetts to Brazil.
Notes: It lives in vertical burrows and has long siphons that extend up to the surface. It is a suspension feeder.

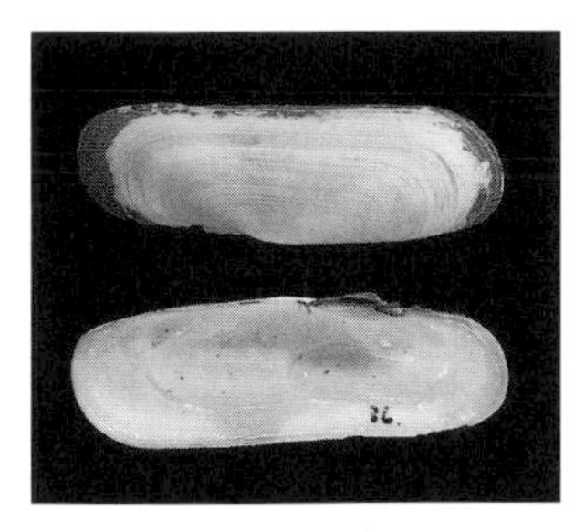

stout tagelus

• **stout tagelus** *Tagelus plebeius* (Lightfoot)
Description: (3 1/2 inches) Strong, stout, rectangular shell resembling the **corrugate solecurtus**. Smooth surface with fine concentric lines not overlain by oblique lines. Beak almost central. Teeth on hinge. No vertical raised rib inside shell as in the **purplish tagelus**. Large pallial sinus.
Color: Whitish exterior with no purplish rays.
Habitat: Lives in sounds. Commonly found washed onto sound and ocean beaches.
Range: Massachusetts to Argentina.
Notes: See **purplish tagelus** *Notes*.

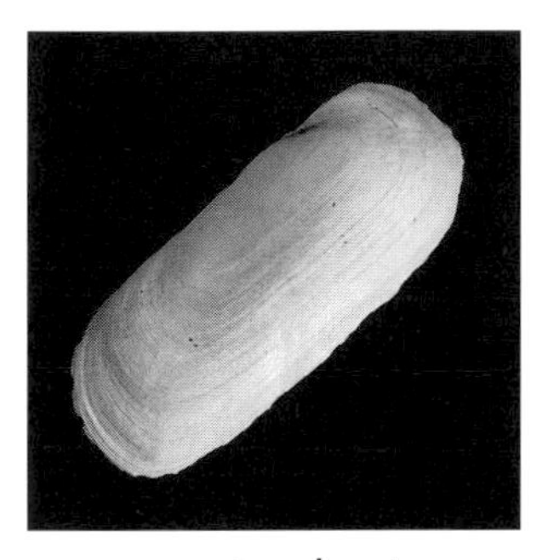

corrugate solecurtus

• **corrugate solecurtus** *Solecurtus cumingianus* Dunker
Description: (2 3/4 inches) Rectangular, gaping shell with bluntly rounded ends. Similar to **stout tagelus** except ends more rounded and the coarse concentric lines overlain by sharp, oblique lines. Beak almost central. Small hinge teeth.
Color: White exterior. Yellowish gray periostracum.
Habitat: Lives offshore in sand or mud. Rarely found on ocean beaches.
Range: North Carolina to Brazil.
Notes: Also called a **corrugated razor clam**. It is able to burrow rapidly into sand.

RAZOR-SHAPED – jackknives (Solenidae)

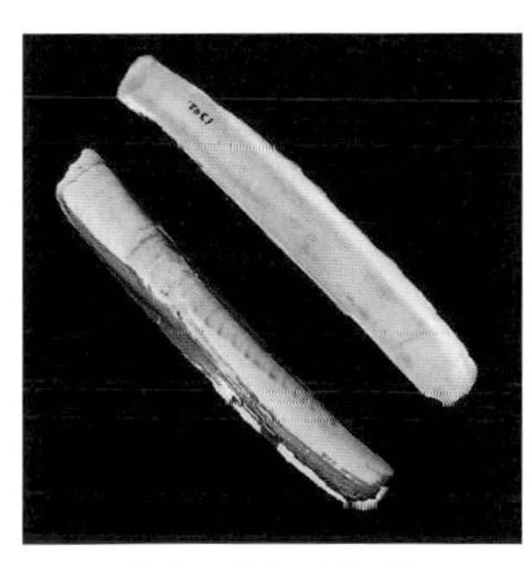

Atlantic jackknife

• **Atlantic jackknife** *Ensis directus* Conrad
Description: (5 inches) Long, slender shell six times as long as high. Slightly curved with blunt ends. Looks like an old-fashioned razor. Cardinal and lateral hinge teeth at back end of beak.
Color: Whitish exterior. White and violet interior. Shiny olive to brown periostracum.
Habitat: Lives in sounds and offshore burrowing in muddy sand. Common on ocean beaches, particularly above Cape Hatteras. Often found in shell drift at tide line.
Range: Canada to South Carolina.
Notes: This species is excellent tasting but not fished commercially. It burrows rapidly into sand and swims in an erratic manner. Edges of the shell are sharp.

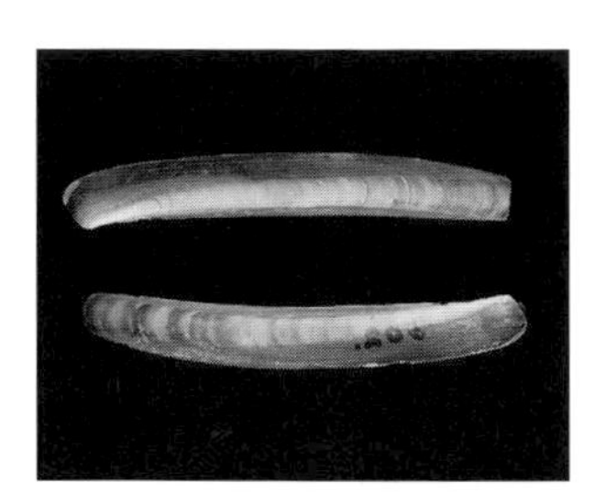

minor jackknife

• **minor jackknife** *Ensis minor* Dall
Description: (5 inches, but most are about 1 3/4 inches) Similar to the **Atlantic jackknife** except smaller, more fragile and possibly more pointed at the toothless end of the hinge. About nine times as long as high.
Color: Whitish exterior. Interior stained with purple. Reportedly paler than the **Atlantic jackknife**.
Habitat: Lives offshore burrowed in muddy sand at depths to about 60 feet and in moderate- to high-salinity estuaries. Commonly washed onto ocean beaches.
Range: New Jersey to Texas.
Notes: Also called a **dwarf razor clam** or **common razor clam**. It is often eaten by wading birds. Authorities question whether this might be a subspecies of the **Atlantic jackknife**. Most small specimens found below the Cape Lookout area should be the **minor jackknife**.

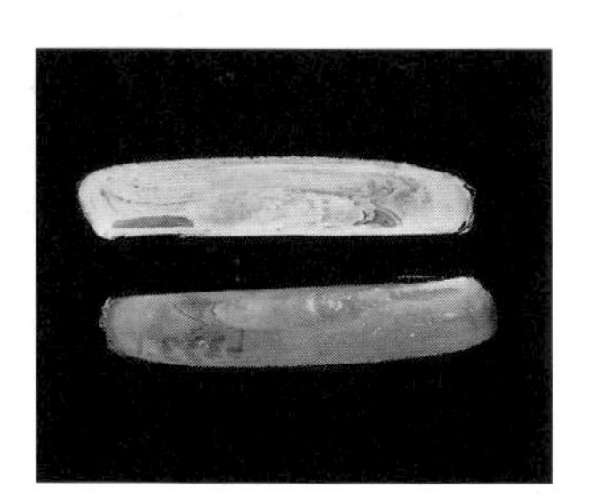

green jackknife

• **green jackknife** *Solen viridis* Say
Description: (1 1/2 inches) Long, slender shell similar to the **Atlantic jackknife** but shorter and less curved. Four or five times as long as high. Hinge line almost straight but possibly slightly curved. One cardinal tooth in hinge of each valve.
Color: Grayish white exterior and interior. Yellowish green periostracum.
Habitat: Lives in sounds and intertidal sand bars. Occasionally washed onto sound and ocean beaches in shell drift at tide line.
Range: Rhode Island to Texas.
Notes: See **Atlantic jackknife** ***Notes***.

RAZOR-SHAPED – awningclams (Solemyidae)

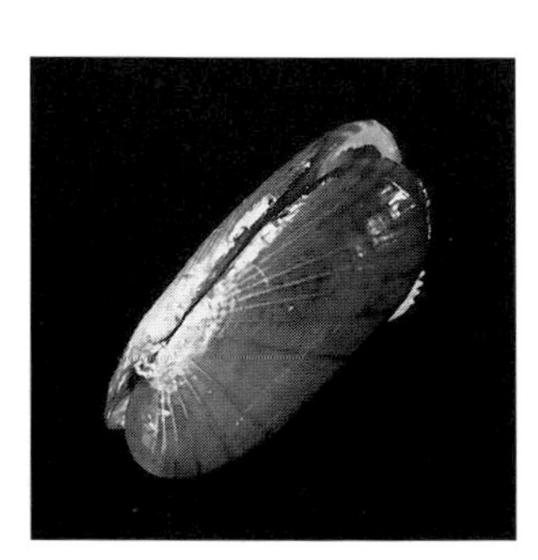

Atlantic awningclam

◊ • **Atlantic awningclam** *Solemya velum* Say
Description: (1 inch) Elongate, smooth and fragile shell more than twice as long as high. Named for tough periostracum extending beyond the shell's edge as if it were an awning or fringe. Beak near one end. No teeth on hinge. Possibly some weak crenulations at bottom edge.
Color: Brown exterior with radial rays appearing light beneath the dark brown periostracum. Grayish white interior.
Habitat: Lives in sounds, burrowed into intertidal sand flats in U-shaped burrows. Rarely washed onto sound beaches.
Range: Nova Scotia, Canada, to Florida.
Notes: Also known as the **veiled clam**. This animal has about 16 appendages on its siphon. It is an active swimmer. It should be stored separately in collections because the awning is fragile.

Gastropods

WHELK-SHAPED – whelks (Melongenidae)

North Carolina waters probably have more whelk species than any other area on the East Coast. The beauty and size of these whelks are striking. North Carolina conch chowder (or Carteret County conch chowder) is made from whelks. In Florida, conch chowder is made from the **queen conch**, a true conch, which is closely related to North Carolina's **Florida fighting conch**. Nomenclature of local whelk species is unsettled and will likely remain so until more research is done.

lightning whelk

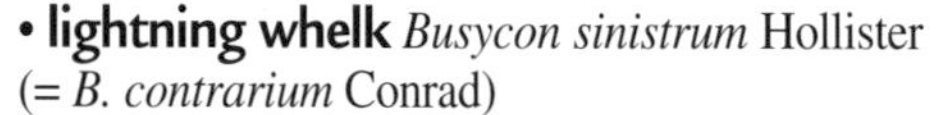

• **lightning whelk** *Busycon sinistrum* Hollister
(= *B. contrarium* Conrad)
Description: (12 1/2 inches) Large, pear-shaped shell. Very similar to the **knobbed whelk** except whorl knobs smaller and aperture on the left (remember: lightning = left). ("Right-handed" specimens sometimes found.) Smooth exterior. Wide aperture ends in a long, straight canal. Smooth inner lip. Horny operculum.
Color: Large specimens (more than 8 to 9 inches) usually dull white on the exterior. Smaller specimens light brown and vertically streaked with darker violet-brown. Yellow to violet tints sometimes in interior (**knobbed whelks** usually more orange).
Habitat: Lives on the sandy bottoms of sounds, inlets and just offshore. Frequently found on sound and ocean beaches.
Range: New Jersey to Florida and Gulf states.
Notes: This animal is a carnivore (a major quahog predator) and scavenger. It uses its strong foot and aperture lip to force apart bivalves or to chip away the shell until it can insert its mouth and feed on the mollusk inside. Females lay disk-shaped egg capsules attached on a string, which are often found washed onto beaches and mistaken for seaweed. Juveniles crawl out of capsules.

knobbed whelk

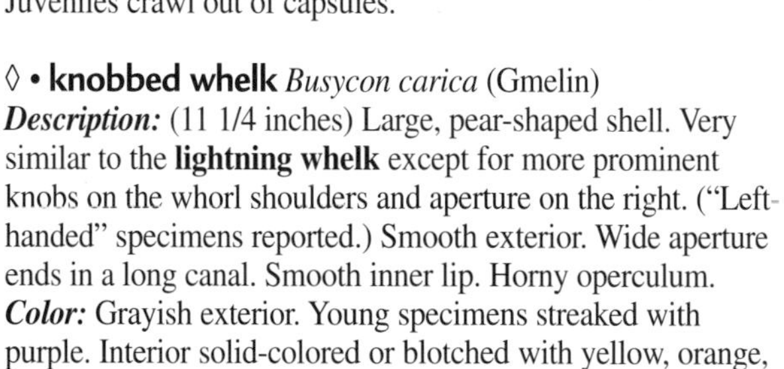

◊ • **knobbed whelk** *Busycon carica* (Gmelin)
Description: (11 1/4 inches) Large, pear-shaped shell. Very similar to the **lightning whelk** except for more prominent knobs on the whorl shoulders and aperture on the right. ("Left-handed" specimens reported.) Smooth exterior. Wide aperture ends in a long canal. Smooth inner lip. Horny operculum.
Color: Grayish exterior. Young specimens streaked with purple. Interior solid-colored or blotched with yellow, orange, red or brown.

Continued on upper right

Continued from lower left

Habitat: Lives in sounds, inlets and shallow offshore waters. Frequently found on sound and ocean beaches.
Range: Massachusetts to Florida.
Notes: This animal is a carnivore (a major clam predator) and scavenger. See **lightning whelk** ***Notes*** for feeding technique and egg capsules. Note egg capsules in the photo.

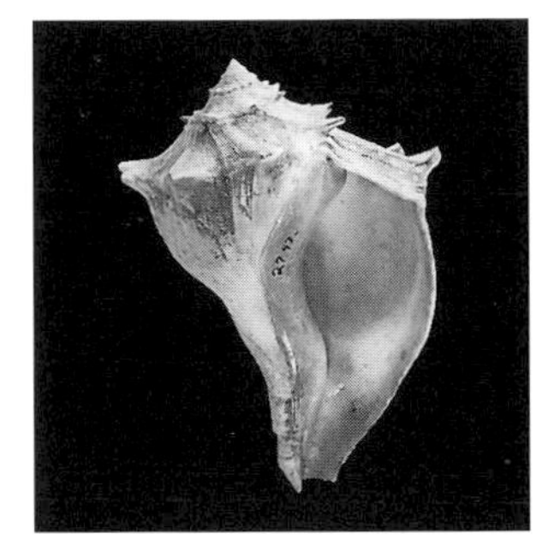

Kiener whelk

* • **Kiener whelk** *Busycon carica eliceans* (Montfort)
Description: (8 inches) Heavy, rough-looking shell very similar to the **knobbed whelk**. Distinguished by a noticeable swelling near the lower part of the body whorl and by heavy, recurved spines on the shoulder.
Color: Gray with brownish purple axial streaks. Inside aperture lip sometimes glazed orange.
Habitat: Lives on sandy bottoms of sounds, inlets and shallow offshore waters. Occasionally washed onto ocean beaches below Cape Fear or found offshore by scuba divers.
Range: South of Cape Fear, N.C., to Florida.
Notes: Do not confuse this species with young **knobbed whelks**, which also have brownish purple streaks. See **lightning whelk** ***Notes*** for feeding technique and egg capsules.

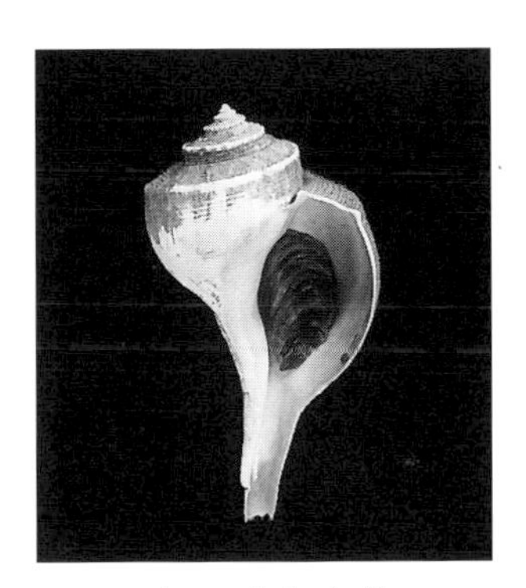

channeled whelk

• **channeled whelk** *Busycotypus canaliculatus* (Linnaeus) (= *Busycon canaliculata*)
Description: (8 1/2 inches) Large, pear-shaped shell with aperture on the right. ("Left-handed" specimens reported.) Fine spiral ridges. Whorl shoulders lack large knobs (shoulders of the earliest whorls beaded). Named for channel at the juncture of each previous whorl. Spire higher than that of the **pearwhelk**. Wide aperture ends in a canal. Smooth inner lip. Horny operculum.
Color: Yellowish white to grayish exterior. Interior shades of yellow, orange or violet.
Habitat: Lives in shallow offshore waters and the deeper areas of sounds and inlets. Occasionally found on sound and ocean beaches.
Range: Massachusetts to Florida.
Notes: This species is a carnivore and scavenger. See **lightning whelk** ***Notes*** on feeding technique and egg capsules.

pearwhelk

• **pearwhelk** *Busycotypus spiratus* (Lamarck) (= *Busycon spiratum pyruloides* Lamarck, *B. pyrum* Dillwyn)
Description: (5 1/4 inches) Large, pear-shaped shell with aperture on right. Very similar to the **Atlantic figsnail** or **fig shell** but no crisscross sculpture and slightly higher spire. No knobs on early whorl shoulders, which are more sloping than those of the **knobbed whelk**. Each succeeding whorl joins previous whorl at its shoulder; on the **channeled whelk**, each whorl forms a sunken channel before attaching to the preceding whorl. Inner aperture lip smooth. Horny operculum.
Color: Cream with broad, brown, spiral bands crossed by thin brown axial streaks.
Habitat: Lives offshore.
Range: North Carolina to Florida.
Notes: Also known as the **fig whelk**, but this species should not be confused with the **Atlantic figsnail**. It is a carnivore and probably a scavenger. See **lightning whelk** ***Notes*** on feeding and egg capsules.

WHELK-SHAPED – figsnails (Ficidae)

Atlantic figsnail

• **Atlantic figsnail** *Ficus communis* Röding
Description: (4 1/2 inches) Smooth, pear-shaped shell with almost no spire. Unlike the **pearwhelk**, has many pronounced spiral ridges crossing finer axial riblets and no operculum. Wide aperture on right runs almost the length of the shell and narrows into a canal. Spiral ridges or folds inside inner lip.
Color: Cream or pinkish gray exterior with brown broken spiral stripes. Glossy tan interior.
Habitat: Lives offshore. Rarely found on ocean beaches.
Range: North Carolina to Mexico.
Notes: Also called a **paper fig shell**. This species is a carnivore. Females lay egg capsules in wide rows. When alive, the mantle almost covers the shell. Do not confuse this shell with the **pearwhelk**.

WHELK-SHAPED – **true conchs** (Strombidae)

Florida fighting conch

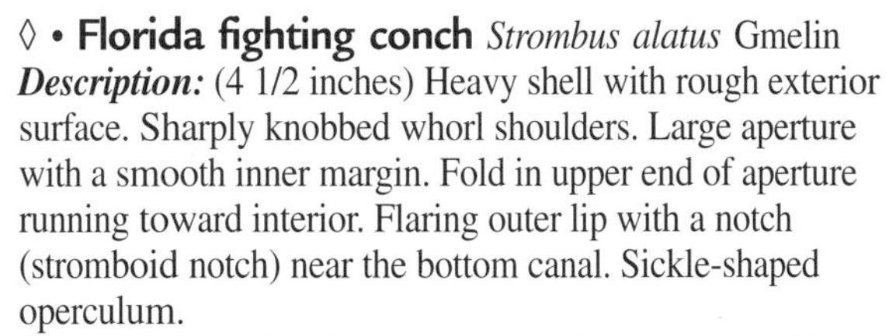

◊ • **Florida fighting conch** *Strombus alatus* Gmelin
Description: (4 1/2 inches) Heavy shell with rough exterior surface. Sharply knobbed whorl shoulders. Large aperture with a smooth inner margin. Fold in upper end of aperture running toward interior. Flaring outer lip with a notch (stromboid notch) near the bottom canal. Sickle-shaped operculum.
Color: Light to dark brown exterior with shiny, metallic parietal shield that may be dark reddish orange to reddish purple. Similarly colored interior but not metallic.
Habitat: Lives offshore, known at depths up to 120 feet. Occasionally washed onto ocean beaches, particularly Cape Lookout and Shackleford Banks.
Range: North Carolina to Texas.
Notes: A herbivore, it feeds on red algae. Females lay long, jellylike strings of eggs that release free-swimming young. Occasionally, it is brought up by offshore fishing trawlers. The tasty meat is eaten as steaks or in chowders and salads. It is closely related to the **queen conch** or **pink conch** (*Stombus gigas* Linnaeus), which is used in conch chowder in Southern states.

milk conch

◊ • **milk conch** *Strombus costatus* Gmelin
Description: (6 inches) Heavy shell with a high spire, similar to the **Florida fighting conch**. Sharp knobs on shoulders of whorls. Low spiral corrugations on body whorl. Outer lip of the long, narrow aperture greatly expands outward. Typical strombid notch on lower canal of aperture. Much thicker shell in older specimens. Thin shell in immature specimens with no outward expanded lip. Thin periostracum when alive.
Color: Yellowish white exterior with light orangish spiral lines. Shiny white aperture. Tan periostracum.
Habitat: Found south of Cape Lookout, living offshore in sand and vegetation at depths of 70 to 80 feet. Possibly lives in shallower waters farther south. Should be collectible by scuba divers.
Range: South of Cape Lookout, N.C., to Florida and Brazil.
Notes: Also called a **ribbed stromb**. This species is a herbivore. Young are free-swimming.

WHELK-SHAPED – tulips (Fasciolariidae)

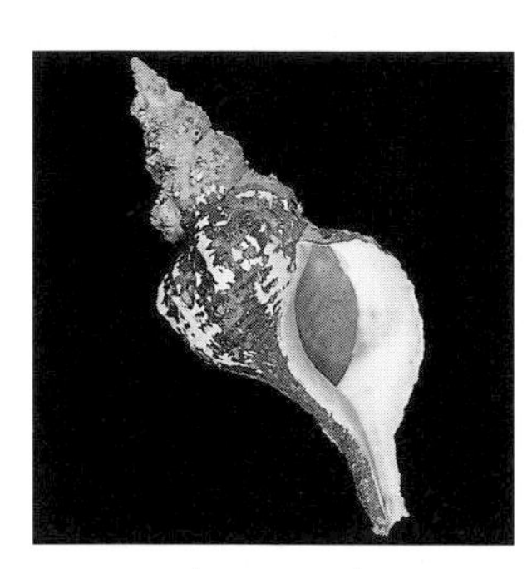

horse conch

• **horse conch** *Pleuroploca gigantea* (Kiener)
Description: (16 1/4 inches) Large, spindle-shaped shell resembling a tulip shell. Rough exterior surface covered by a flaky periostracum. No extra large ribs. Large aperture with a long lower canal. Spiral ridges on inner lip run into the interior. Large, horny operculum.
Color: Cream or orange exterior and interior. Exterior covered with a dark brown periostracum (dark orange, red or brown on small specimens).
Habitat: Lives offshore. Rarely washed onto ocean beaches.
Range: North Carolina to Mexico.
Notes: One of the largest living gastropods, this species is known to reach more than 19 inches in length. The meat is orange and peppery-tasting. A carnivore, it feeds on large gastropods (its favorite prey) while holding the victim's operculum to prevent it from closing. Females lay groups of funnel-shaped, ridged egg capsules, each about 1 inch long. Hatched young crawl away. This species is closely related to tulip shells. It was named Florida's state shell in 1969.

banded tulip

◊ * • **banded tulip** *Fasciolaria lilium hunteria* (G. Perry)
Description: (4 1/2 inches) Spindle-shaped shell resembling the **true tulip** except smaller. Smooth and shiny exterior. Smooth sutures between whorls. High spire. Teardrop-shaped aperture with fold at the upper canal and one or two folds on the lower inner portion. Horny operculum.
Color: Cream background mottled with brown (or sometimes with gray or blue-green). Thin, dark brown lines spiraling around shell do not run into aperture.
Habitat: Lives in sounds and offshore, frequently on pilings or shelly substrate. Occasionally found on sound and ocean beaches.
Range: North Carolina to Texas.
Notes: This species is more common in North Carolina than the **true tulip**. A carnivore, it actively searches for other mollusks. It prefers gastropods, such as the **Atlantic oyster drill**, but it will eat bivalves. It uses its foot to pry open bivalves, then wedges its aperture lip inside to feed on the animal's soft parts. Females lay eggs in funnel-shaped capsules attached to rocks or shells. Hatched young crawl away.

true tulip

◊ • **true tulip** *Fasciolaria tulipa* (Linnaeus)
Description: (9 1/2 inches) Large, spindle-shaped shell resembling the banded tulip but larger, with rough sutures between whorls. Rough spiral cords just below sutures. Smooth and shiny exterior. High spire. Teardrop-shaped aperture with a fold at the upper canal and one or two folds on the lower inside portion. Horny operculum.
Color: Cream to pink background with brown spiral bands and many darker and broken spiral lines running into aperture.
Habitat: Lives offshore. Live specimens found in Cape Lookout Bight.
Range: North Carolina to Brazil.
Notes: A carnivore, it actively searches for mollusks, especially large gastropods. Females lay eggs in funnel-shaped capsules attached to rocks or shells. Hatched young crawl away.

WHELK-SHAPED – tritons (Ranellidae) (= Cymatiidae)

Kreb triton

◊ * • **Kreb triton** *Cymatium corrugatum krebsii* (Morch)
Description: (2 3/4 inches) Resembles a murex shell. Spire less than twice the aperture length. Whorls of spire joined in a tight coil. Last whorl has six to seven heavy spiral cords and one large, thickened axial rib (in addition to the heavy outer lip of the aperture). Six to seven strong teeth on outer lip. Two large folds on inner margin and smaller folds running into aperture. Operculum.
Color: White exterior. Light brown periostracum.
Habitat: Lives offshore, particularly near **Atlantic calico scallop** beds.
Range: North Carolina to West Indies.
Notes: A carnivore, it anesthetizes its prey with a secretion, then inserts its mouth inside the shell to feed. Females lay small, round egg capsules on hard surfaces. Young are free-swimming. A one- to two-month swimming stage allows considerable dispersal of the species. Very few tritons have been found in North Carolina waters except during the early 1970s as part of the **Atlantic calico scallop** fishery.

Poulsen triton

* • **Poulsen triton** *Cymatium cingulatum* (Lamarck) (= *C. poulsenii* Morch)
Description: (2 3/4 inches) Murexlike shell with a moderate spire. Shouldered whorls. Last whorl slightly shouldered with 18 to 20 strong spiral cords. No axial ribs. Wide aperture. Smooth inner margin with a slight fold near the lower canal. Outer aperture lip not thick but slightly flared out. Thin shell with thin periostracum.
Color: White exterior. Brown periostracum.
Habitat: Lives offshore.
Range: Virginia to Brazil.
Notes: See **Kreb triton** *Notes*. No living specimens are known to have been found in North Carolina waters.

giant triton

• **giant triton** *Cymatium parthenopeum* (von Salis)
Description: (6 inches) Murexlike shell with prominent spiral cords. Two strong spiral cords on whorl above the body whorl. Wide aperture with a strong inner fold at the upper canal. Spiral ridges on inner lip that run into the interior. Thick and knobby outer lip where the ribs end. Thick and hairy periostracum (as shown). Operculum.
Color: Brownish yellow exterior with some darker brown spiral bands, particularly on the outer lip. Inner margin of aperture orange to reddish brown with white folds.
Habitat: Lives offshore.
Range: North Carolina to Uruguay.
Notes: Also called a **neapolitan triton**. This species is present in Pacific waters as well. See **Kreb triton** *Notes*. It was frequently found in catches of the **Atlantic calico scallop** fishery.

Atlantic trumpet triton

◊ • **Atlantic trumpet triton** *Charonia tritonis variegata* (Lamarck)
Description: (10 inches) Large, graceful, elongate shell with a high spire and wide aperture. Eight or nine whorls on spire. Spire longer than the aperture. Shoulder of the body whorl slightly angular. Small pairs of teeth on outer aperture lip. Ridged inner lip.
Color: Cream exterior with concentric patterns of brown, purple or red, suggesting the plumage of a pheasant. Orange interior. On aperture, outer lip teeth and inner lip ridges white.
Habitat: Living specimens found by scuba divers off Beaufort Inlet at 60- to 100-foot depths on rocky or shelly substrate near rock outcroppings.
Range: North Carolina to Florida and Brazil.
Notes: Also called a **trumpet shell**. This species has been known to feed on sea stars and sand dollars. Also see **Kreb triton** *Notes*.

Atlantic distortio

• Atlantic distortio *Distortio clathrata* (Lamarck)
Description: (2 3/4 inches) Murexlike shell with a distorted appearance. Knobby, checkerboard appearance on surface created by many axial and spiral ribs. Narrow aperture with large canal-like depression on inner lip. Both lips heavily ridged. Large, shiny parietal shield. Hairy periostracum. Small operculum.
Color: White exterior with some yellow, pink or brown. Brown satinlike periostracum with some bristles.
Habitat: Lives offshore, south of Cape Hatteras to 200-foot depths. Rarely washed onto ocean beaches.
Range: North Carolina to Florida and Brazil.
Notes: Also called a **writhing shell**. See **Kreb triton** *Notes*. The distortio's large aperture teeth and narrow aperture opening give it more protection from predators than most tritons have. A similar but more distorted species, the **McGinty distortio** (*Distortio constricta macgintyi* Emerson and Puffer), is occasionally found farther offshore.

WHELK-SHAPED – murexes (Muricidae)

Atlantic oyster drill

• Atlantic oyster drill *Urosalpinx cinerea* (Say)
Description: (1 1/2 inches) Rough exterior. Nine to 12 large axial ribs, all equal in size, form a pattern of raised wavy lines. Less prominent spiral ridges cross the ribs. Rounded whorls. Wide aperture with a short, open lower canal. Smooth inner lip. Operculum.
Color: Gray exterior, sometimes with light banding. Interior often violet or brownish.
Habitat: Lives in sounds and inlets, in and just below the intertidal zone. Commonly found living on pilings, rock jetties and oyster reefs. Frequently found on sound and ocean beaches.
Range: Nova Scotia, Canada, to Florida.
Notes: This species is a major oyster predator. Its effect on the North Carolina oyster industry is less devastating than in Northern states. A carnivore, it actually prefers barnacles to oysters. It also feeds on other bivalves, gastropods and crabs. It uses its radula to drill an unbeveled hole into the shell and feed on the soft parts. Females lay rounded, funnel-shaped egg capsules on hard surfaces throughout the summer. Hatched young crawl away.

thick-lip drill

• **thick-lip drill** *Eupleura caudata* (Say)
Description: (1 1/2 inches) Rough exterior with strong spiral lines and large axial ribs. Two ribs stronger than the others, giving the shell a flattened appearance. Sharply angled shoulders on whorl. Wide aperture with a long lower canal. Smooth inner lip. Outer lip thick and toothed. Operculum.
Color: White exterior. Occasionally whorls have several purple spiral bands.
Habitat: Lives in sounds, inlets and just offshore, usually near oyster beds, on shelly substrate. Frequently found on sound and ocean beaches.
Range: Massachusetts to Florida.
Notes: Also called a **thick-lipped oyster drill**. A carnivore, it feeds on oysters and other mollusks. This species is a major oyster predator farther north. In late winter and spring, females lay eggs in slender funnel-shaped capsules that have a slender stalk. Hatched young crawl away.

Florida rocksnail

• **Florida rocksnail** *Thais haemastoma floridana* (Conrad)
Description: (3 3/4 inches) Medium-sized shell with a rough surface. Strong spiral lines. Sloped whorl shoulders may have rows of knobs on them and just below. Wide aperture with short, narrow upper canal and short, wide lower canal. Smooth inner lip. Thick, toothed outer lip. No parietal shield. Horny operculum.
Color: Exterior gray to yellow with some brown spiral markings. Interior yellow-orange to pink.
Habitat: Lives near or on rock jetties and oyster beds near inlets. Populous near Ocracoke. Occasionally found on ocean beaches.
Range: Virginia to Brazil.
Notes: Also called a **southern oyster drill**. A carnivore, it feeds on oysters and other mollusks. It is less of a threat to the oyster industry in North Carolina than in the Gulf of Mexico. Females lay funnel-shaped egg capsules. Young are free-swimming. When irritated, this mollusk can exude a poisonous, milky froth that turns purple. Its young, frequently confused with **tinted cantharus**, can be separated by color.

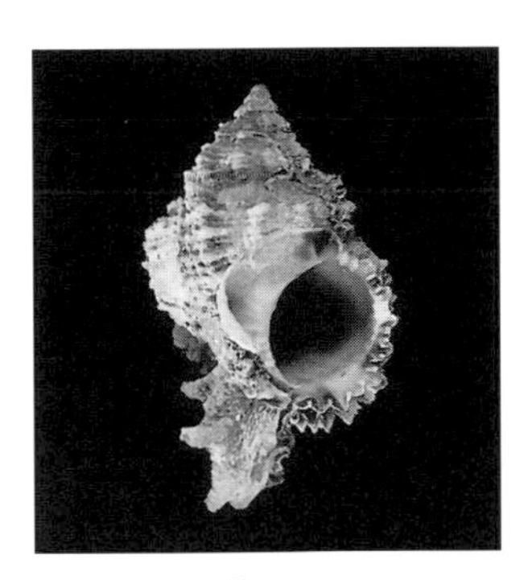

apple murex

• **apple murex** *Phyllonotus pomum* (Gmelin)
(= *Murex pomum*)
Description: (3 1/2 inches) Rough exterior. Three axial ribs stronger than other ribs and have short spines. Rough spiral cords. Wide, round aperture with long, slitlike canal that is nearly closed. Smooth inner lip. Thick outer lip. Horny operculum.
Color: Exterior gray to reddish brown, sometimes with dark spiral stripes or mottling. Interior pinkish with four dark brown spots inside the outer lip.
Habitat: Lives offshore. Common in offshore **Atlantic calico scallop** beds. Rarely washed onto ocean beaches.
Range: North Carolina to Brazil.
Notes: A carnivore, it uses radula and secretions to bore round holes into **eastern oyster** and other bivalve shells. Females lay ball-like masses of tongue-shaped egg capsules under rocks and on shells in early summer. Hatched young crawl away.

lace murex

• **lace murex** *Chicoreus florifer dilectus* A. Adams
(= *Murex dilectus*)
Description: (2 3/4 inches) Rough exterior. Three axial ribs with long, lacelike spines stronger than other ribs. Spiral cords. Wide aperture with a long, slitlike lower canal. Smooth inner lip. Horny operculum.
Color: Cream or light brown exterior, sometimes with fine darker brown spiral lines. Pinkish apex.
Habitat: Lives offshore. Has been found associated with **Atlantic calico scallop** beds.
Range: North Carolina to West Indies.
Notes: A carnivore, it bores holes into bivalve shells and feeds on the soft parts. Females lay egg capsules under rocks and on shells in early summer. Hatched young crawl away. The subspecies *dilectus* is found in North Carolina.

lightweight murex

• **lightweight murex** *Murexiella levicula* (Dall)
(= *Murex leviculus*)
Description: (3/4 inch) Small shell. Five or more large axial ribs with erect spines. Shoulder spines curve upward like a hook. Smooth spaces between ribs. Wide aperture with lower canal that is a long slit. Smooth inner lip. Operculum.
Color: Light brown exterior.
Habitat: Known living offshore in **Atlantic calico scallop** beds.
Range: North Carolina to Florida.
Notes: This species may be easily overlooked because of its small size. It probably has crawl-away young.

giant eastern murex

• **giant eastern murex** *Muricanthus fulvescens* (Sowerby) (= *Murex fulvescens*)
Description: (7 inches) Large, heavy shell with rough surface. Six to 10 axial ribs on each whorl bearing prominent, erect spines. Raised spiral ridges between axial ribs. Long lower canal on aperture. Smooth inner lip. Heavy operculum.
Color: Exterior white, yellow-brown or gray with fine purple spiral lines. Interior white and porcelaneous. Dark operculum.
Habitat: Lives offshore, particularly near **Atlantic calico scallop** beds.
Range: North Carolina to Texas.
Notes: Also called a **tawny murex**. A carnivore, it feeds on bivalves. Females lay large numbers of egg capsules in single-layer mats on hard surfaces (frequently on other **giant eastern murex** shells). It probably has crawl-away young.

pitted murex

• **pitted murex** *Favartia cellulosa* (Conrad)
Description: (3/4 inch) Similar to **lightweight murex** except shoulders of the large axial ribs lack spines, and spaces between the large ribs not smooth but crossed by about five scaly cords.
Color: Light grayish pink to light brown exterior.
Habitat: Lives offshore near **Atlantic calico scallop** beds. Found by scuba divers.
Range: North Carolina to Gulf of Mexico and Brazil.
Notes: A carnivore, it is thought to feed on small, thin-shelled bivalves. It probably has crawl-away young.

AUGER-SHAPED – augers (Terebridae)

eastern auger

◊ • **eastern auger** *Terebra dislocata* (Say)
Description: (2 1/4 inches) Long, pointed spire. Whorls not concave. Prominent spiral cord at top of each whorl that winds around 20 to 25 low axial ribs. Smaller spiral cords between axial ribs. Canal at bottom of aperture. Thin operculum.
Color: Varied exterior with bands of pale gray, pinkish brown or orange-brown. Tan operculum.
Habitat: Lives in sounds and offshore on shallow sand flats. Common on sound and ocean beaches.
Range: Virginia to Brazil.
Notes: Also called a **common American auger** or **Atlantic auger**. A carnivore, it lacks the radula and poison gland found in most other augers. Hatched young crawl away.

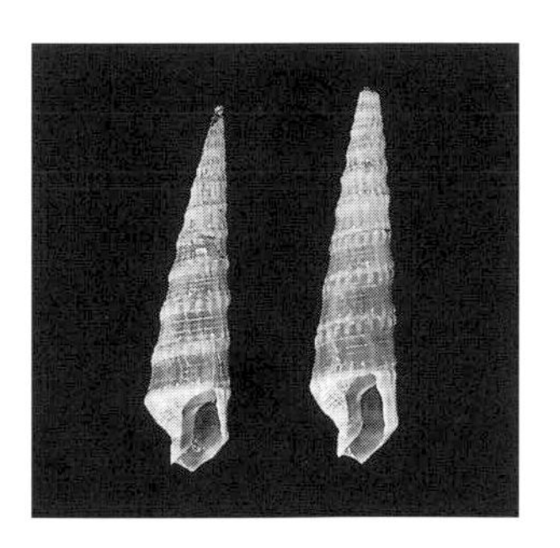
concave auger

• **concave auger** *Terebra concava* (Say)
Description: (1 inch) Long, slender spire. Similar to **eastern auger** except for concave whorls. Beaded spiral rows. Canal at bottom of aperture. Thin operculum.
Color: Yellowish gray exterior. Tan operculum.
Habitat: Occasionally washed onto ocean beaches.
Range: North Carolina to Brazil.
Notes: Hatched young crawl away.

AUGER-SHAPED – turretsnails (Turritellidae)

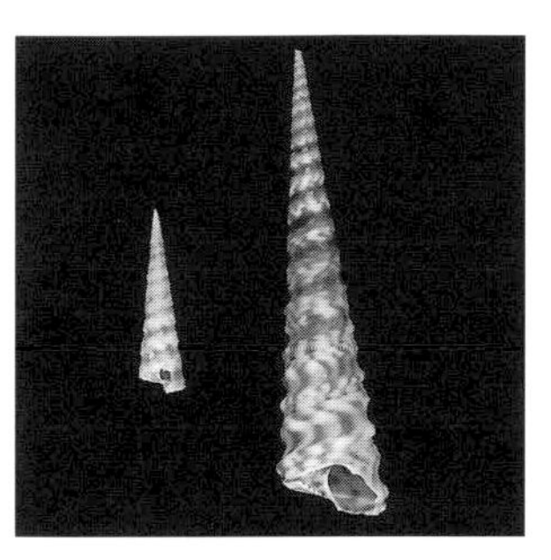
eastern turretsnail

◊ • **eastern turretsnail** *Turritella exoleta* (Linnaeus) (= *Torcula exoleta*)
Description: (2 3/4 inches) Small, slender, tightly coiled shell with a high, sharply pointed spire. Strong, smooth spiral cord at top and bottom of each whorl and concave between. Round aperture with a thin lip. Bristles on edge of operculum.
Color: Whitish exterior with brownish markings.
Habitat: Lives in deep offshore waters.
Range: North Carolina to Brazil.
Notes: Also called a **common turret shell**. This species is a filter feeder.

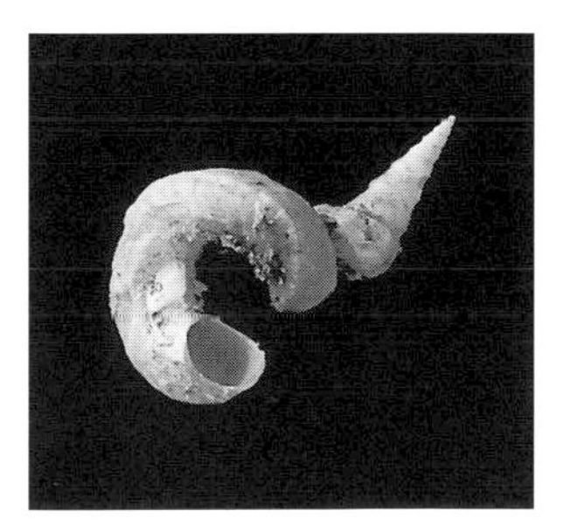
Florida wormsnail

• **Florida wormsnail** *Vermicularia knorri* (Deshayes)
Description: (tight coil: 1/2 inch) Tightly coiled shell apex. Later whorls loose and coil without apparent direction.
Color: Exterior whitish near tip and yellowish brown elsewhere.
Habitat: Lives offshore. Occasionally washed onto ocean beaches.
Range: North Carolina to Gulf of Mexico.
Notes: Also called **Knorr's worm shell**. Shells may become entangled with others and produce a large, worm-shaped mass. This species is a filter feeder.

AUGER-SHAPED – wentletraps (Epitoniidae)

• **brown-band wentletrap** *Epitonium rupicola* (Kurtz)
Description: (1/2 inch) Small shell with a high, sharply pointed spire composed of globose whorls. About 12 to 18 weak ribs on each whorl. Smooth spaces between ribs. Round aperture. Operculum.

Continued on next page

brown-band wentletrap

Continued from previous page

Color: Whitish exterior with brown spiral bands. Two brown bands on body whorl. Mahogany-colored operculum.
Habitat: Lives in sounds and just offshore. Occasionally washed onto sound and ocean beaches, usually in drift at the tide line. Easily overlooked because of its small size.
Range: Massachusetts to Texas.
Notes: Also called a **lined wentletrap**. About 24 kinds of wentletraps have been recorded in North Carolina waters. A carnivore, it forages in sand for sea anemones and tears tissue with its jaws. It secretes a substance that turns purple and may anesthetize the anemones. Females lays strings of sand-covered egg capsules. Its young are free-swimming. The **precious wentletrap** (up to 2 3/4 inches long) from the Pacific Ocean is one of the prettiest shells known.

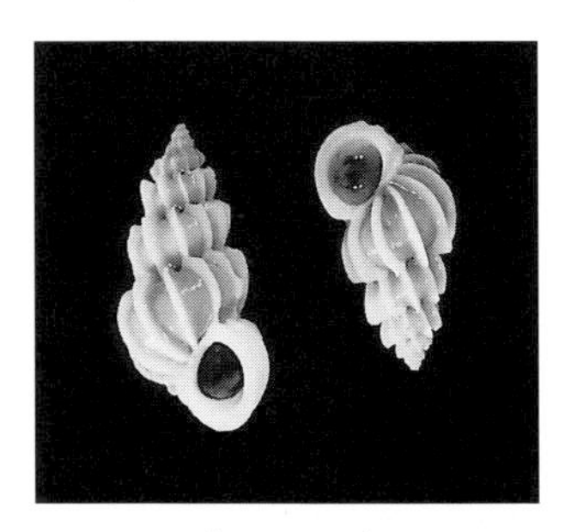

angulate wentletrap

• **angulate wentletrap** *Epitonium angulatum* (Say)
Description: (1 inch) High, slender, glossy spire. Each whorl with nine to 10 strong ribs, each slightly angled on the whorl shoulder. Smooth spaces between ribs. Round aperture. Operculum.
Color: Shiny white interior and exterior. Reddish brown operculum.
Habitat: Occasionally found in drift on ocean beaches.
Range: New York to Uruguay.
Notes: See **brown-band wentletrap** ***Notes***.

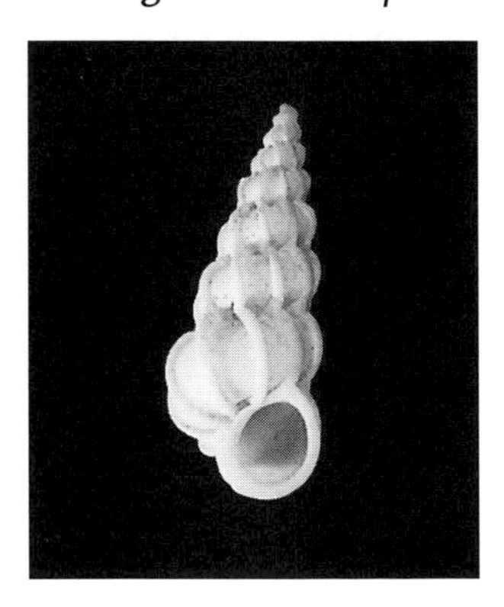

Humphrey wentletrap

* • **Humphrey wentletrap** *Epitonium humphreysii* (Kiener)
Description: (3/4 inch) Small, high-spired shell. Very similar to **angulate wentletrap** in appearance, habitat and numbers, but eight to nine rounded ribs on each whorl thicker and not angulate at shoulder. Also, generally more slender with a thicker lip on round aperture. Smooth spaces between ribs. Operculum.
Color: White exterior and interior. Mahogany-colored operculum.
Habitat: Occasionally found in drift on ocean beaches.
Range: Massachusetts to Texas.
Notes: See **brown-band wentletrap** ***Notes***.

many-rib wentletrap

reticulate wentletrap

dark cerith

• **many-rib wentletrap** *Epitonium multistriatum* (Say)
Description: (1/2 inch) Small, fragile, high-spired shell with seven or eight whorls. Similar to **angulate wentletrap** except smaller, and ribs noticeably thinner and closer together. Sixteen to 19 ribs on body whorl of adult. Very fine spiral ribbing. Oval aperture with thin lip.
Color: Dull white exterior and interior.
Habitat: Occasionally found in drift on ocean beaches.
Range: Massachusetts to Florida and Texas.
Notes: See **brown-band wentletrap** *Notes*.

• **reticulate wentletrap** *Amaea retifera* (Dall)
Description: (1 inch) High, slender spire. Network pattern on surface created by many bladelike ribs that cross spiral ridges. Ridges weaker than ribs. Round aperture. Operculum.
Color: Straw-yellow to pale brown exterior, some with dark spots.
Habitat: Lives offshore.
Range: North Carolina to Brazil.
Notes: See **brown-band wentletrap** *Notes*.

AUGER-SHAPED – ceriths (Cerithiidae)

• **dark cerith** *Cerithium atratum* (Born)
(= *C. floridanum* Morch)
Description: (1 3/4 inches) Slender, high-spired, heavy-looking shell. Knobby, well-beaded spiral lines more prominent than axial ribs. Canal at bottom of aperture. Small operculum.
Color: Cream exterior stained with brownish gray.
Habitat: Lives in sounds and near inlets south of Cape Hatteras. Occasionally washed onto beaches.
Range: North Carolina to Brazil.
Notes: Also called a **Florida cerith** or **Florida horn shell**. This species feeds on detritus and algae on rocks or sand. Young are probably free-swimming.

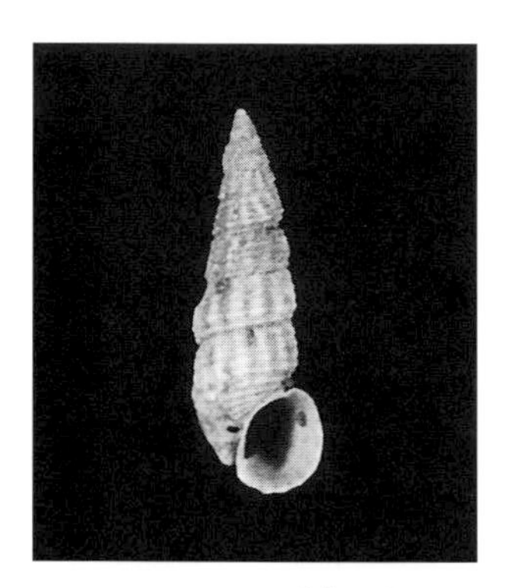
grass cerith

• **grass cerith** *Bittium varium* (Pfeiffer) (= *Diastoma varium*)
Description: (1/4 inch) Very small shell. A long, slender spire. Network pattern on surface created by spiral lines crossing vertical ribs. Usually one thickened rib on body whorl.
Color: Grayish brown and white exterior.
Habitat: Lives in high-salinity estuaries.
Range: Canada to Brazil.
Notes: Also called a **variable bittum**. This species is commonly seen crawling on hard substrates during early summer. It feeds on detritus and algae.

AUGER-SHAPED – miniature ceriths (Cerithiopsidae)

Adam's miniature cerith

* • **Adam's miniature cerith** *Seila adamsi* (H.C. Lea)
Description: (3/8 inch) Small, slender shell. Flat whorls, each with three raised spiral threads. About three, smooth, glassy early whorls. Smooth, concave base. Aperture length about one-fifth of total shell length. Short, twisted, open canal.
Color: Dark brown to orangish brown.
Habitat: Lives offshore to depths of about 100 feet and occasionally on shelly bottoms of high-salinity estuaries such as Bogue Sound and Beaufort Inlet. Commonly washed onto ocean beaches.
Range: Massachusetts to Florida, Texas and Brazil.
Notes: Also called a **wood screw shell**.

AUGER-SHAPED – pyrams (Pyramidellidae)

half-smooth odostome

• **half-smooth odostome** *Boonea seminuda* (C.B. Adams) (= *Odostomia seminuda*)
Description: (less than 1/4 inch) Very small shell with a high spire. Four to six strong spiral cords on whorls crossed by equally strong axial ribs, creating a waffled appearance. Only the spiral cords strong on the whorl base. Oval aperture almost half the length of the shell.
Color: White.
Habitat: Lives in estuaries and offshore waters. Occasionally found on sound and ocean beaches.
Range: Nova Scotia, Canada, to Florida and Texas.
Notes: A parasite, it uses a piercing spine and long proboscis to suck up fluids and soft tissue at the valve edges of **Atlantic bay scallops** and **Atlantic calico scallops**. When a scallop's valves are slightly open, the snail will feed on its mantle tissue. It also may feed on slippersnails.

impressed odostome

• impressed odostome *Boonea impressa* (Say)
(= *Odostomia impressa*)
Description: (less than 1/4 inch) Very small shell with a high spire. Three or four strong spiral cords on each of the six or seven whorls. Oval aperture about one-third the length of the shell.
Color: Milky white.
Habitat: Lives in estuaries, often feeding on **eastern oysters**. Occasionally found on sound and ocean beaches.
Range: Massachusetts to Florida and Gulf of Mexico.
Notes: A parasite, it uses its proboscis and spine to feed on the mantle tissue of oysters when their valves are slightly open. If too many are feeding on one oyster, the oyster's condition can become weakened. This species also may feed on sea squirts (tunicates).

crenulated pyram

* **• crenulated pyram** *Pyramidella crenulata* (Holmes)
Description: (1/2 inch) Slender, conical shell with a spire about three to four times the aperture length. About 12 smooth, flat whorls with deeply channeled sutures. Body whorl slightly angular at one end. Oval aperture. Horny operculum.
Color: Cream with tan blotches.
Habitat: Lives in high-salinity estuaries and on offshore sandy bottoms. Can be commonly found washed onto beaches below Cape Hatteras.
Range: North Carolina to Florida and Texas.
Notes: A parasite, it uses its proboscis and spine to feed on soft tissues of mollusks and other marine animals.

AUGER-SHAPED – turrids (Turridae)

white-band drillia

• white-band drillia *Pilsbryspira albomaculata* (d'Orbigny) (?= *Crassispira albomaculata*)
Description: (3/8 inch) Chunky, spindle-shaped shell with a spire about two-thirds the total shell length. About two spiral cords on each whorl — lower cord larger and knobbed. Spiral cords that reach from shoulder of the body whorl to upper canal of the narrow aperture. Deep, almost closed, tubular notch at upper end of aperture (turrid notch).
Color: Dark-brown shell with a whitish or yellowish band (following the knobbed spiral cord).
Habitat: Known in North Carolina waters at depths of 35 to 55 feet. Found by scuba divers with **lions-paw scallops** in the offshore Cape Fear area. Rare on ocean beaches.

Continued on next page

Continued from previous page

Range: Cape Lookout, N.C., to Florida, Texas and West Indies.
Notes: Turrids, like cone shells, have a radula with poisonous dartlike teeth. These teeth are not known to be poisonous to humans but are used on the animal's prey — in this case, polychaete worms.

cydia drillia

* • **cydia drillia** *Drillia cydia* (Bartsch) (= *Neodrillia cydia*)
Description: (1/2 inch) Spindle-shaped shell with a long, narrow spire about two-thirds the total shell length. Whorls with six to nine distinct axial ribs that are blunt to rounded. Distinct, crowded spiral lines cross axial ribs and spaces between the ribs. Two and a half smooth whorls on nuclear whorl. Narrow aperture with a deep, almost tubular turrid notch just under the body whorl suture and an open lower canal.
Color: White. Sometimes a row of brown spots at the base of the axial ribs.
Habitat: Known offshore of Cape Lookout and Cape Fear at 70- to 300-foot depths. Has been collected from **Atlantic calico scallop** beds and by scuba divers on sandy bottom at 80-foot depths off Wrightsville Beach.
Range: South of Cape Lookout, N.C., to Florida and West Indies.
Notes: Also called a **cydia turret**, **glorious drillia** or **glorious neodrillia**. Its feeding technique is similar to the **white-band drillia** except its prey are sipunculid worms.

Simpson drillia

◊ * • **Simpson drillia** *Cerodrillia simpsoni* (Dall in Simpson)
Description: (1/4 inch) Small, spindle-shaped shell with a long, narrow spire about three-fourths the total shell length. About nine smooth, oily, axial ribs on each whorl. Axial ribs rounded, slightly S-shaped and highest just above the lower whorl suture. Narrow aperture with a moderately deep turrid notch under the body whorl suture and a short lower canal.
Color: Dead shells white to pink. Live specimens bright red.
Habitat: Has been found living south of Cape Hatteras near **Atlantic calico scallops**.
Range: North Carolina to Gulf of Mexico.
Notes: Frequently found in the stomach of the sea star, *Astropecten articulatus*. Also see **white-band drillia** ***Notes***.

reddish mangelia

• **reddish mangelia** *Kurtziella rubella* (Kurtz & Stimpson)
Description: (3/8 inch) Spindle-shaped shell with a moderately high spire just more than half the total shell length. Shell's width about one-third its length. Two smooth nuclear whorls. Eight to nine obtusely angled, slightly S-shaped axial ribs on the surface that are covered by crowded microscopic spiral threads. Axial ribs extend from body whorl to just above the aperture's lower canal. Long, narrow aperture with a shallow turrid notch and a somewhat lengthened lower canal.
Color: Grayish cream with a wide spiral band of light to dark red just below the whorl suture. Several similar bands below shoulder on body whorl.
Habitat: Lives offshore to depths of 50 feet or more. Has been found on **Atlantic calico scallop** beds. Occasionally washed onto ocean beaches south of Cape Hatteras.
Range: North Carolina to Florida and Texas.
Notes: This species is found in the stomach of the sea star *Astropecten articulatus*. See **white-band drillia** ***Notes***.

waxy mangelia

• **waxy mangelia** *Cryoturris cerinella* (Dall)
Description: (1/4 inch) Small, narrow, spindle-shaped shell with a spire two-thirds the total shell length. Whorl of fine axial riblets following two smooth, rounded nuclear whorls. Seven to nine moderately sized and obtusely angled axial ribs on each whorl. These ribs are crossed by crowded microscopically beaded spiral lines. Several stronger, threadlike spiral lines on each whorl. Narrow aperture with a shallow turrid notch and a short lower canal.
Color: Yellowish white. Crowded, microscopically beaded spiral lines that make the whorl surface appear frosted.
Habitat: Found living south of Cape Lookout at 30- to 70-foot depths. Occasionally washed onto ocean beaches south of Cape Lookout. Also found on **Atlantic calico scallop** beds.
Range: North Carolina to Florida and Texas.
Notes: This species is difficult to distinguish from other small turrids in North Carolina waters, such as the **yellow mangelia**, *Cryoturris citronella* (Dall), the *__Fargo mangelia__, *C. fargoi* McGinty, and the **punctate mangelia**, *Kurtziella limonitella* (Dall). It is often found in the stomach of the sea star, *Astropecten articulatus*. See **white-band drillia** ***Notes*** for feeding method.

plicate mangelia

• **plicate mangelia** *Pyrgocythara plicosa* (C.B. Adams) (= *Mangelia plicosa*)
Description: (1/4 inch) Small, stubby, spindle-shaped shell. About nine strong, rounded axial ribs crossed by three to four slightly weaker spiral ribs — a pattern than continues on the body whorl to the upper aperture canal. U-shaped, moderately deep turrid notch on narrow aperture. Often, the aperture's outer lip and the upper notch thicken into a large rib. Aperture length about equal to the shell width and slightly less than half the total shell length.
Color: White to reddish brown.
Habitat: Lives in moderate- to high-salinity estuaries, often associated with eelgrass beds. Rarely found offshore. Occasionally washed onto ocean and sound beaches.
Range: Cape Cod, Mass., to Florida and Texas.
Notes: Also called a **plicate turret shell**. See **white-band drillia** *Notes*.

smooth oxia

* • **smooth oxia** *Nannodiella oxia* (Bush)
Description: (3/16 inch) Small, sharp, spindle-shaped shell with a high spire two-thirds the total shell length. Sharp nuclear whorl with at least three smooth translucent whorls and one whorl with a single raised spiral line. Crisscross appearance on each whorl caused at junctures where spiral and axial threads cross, creating sharp nodules. Spaces between the spiral and axial threads squarish and smooth to shiny. Beaded spiral lines on base of body whorl. Deep U-shaped turrid notch and moderately long lower canal on narrow aperture. Often the aperture's outer lip and bottom notch thicken into a large rib.
Color: White to light pink. Possibly light pink spiral bands.
Habitat: Lives offshore Cape Hatteras and south at depths of 100 feet and more. Known living on **Atlantic calico scallop** beds. Occasionally washed onto ocean beaches.
Range: North Carolina to Florida and Yucatan.
Notes: This species is found in the stomach of the sea star, *Astropecten articulatus*. See **white-band drillia** *Notes*.

AUGER-SHAPED – eulimas (Eulimidae)

brown-line niso

◊ • **brown-line niso** *Niso aeglees* Bush
Description: (1/2 inch) Acutely cone-shaped shell with flat-sided whorls. Angled shoulder of body whorl. Aperture length less than half the total shell length. Broadly ovate aperture. Deep, funnel-like umbilicus.
Color: Shiny, light brown whorls. A narrow dark line on all whorl sutures, the angled shoulder of the body whorl and the angled shoulder of the umbilicus. May have dark brown axial flammules on whorls.
Habitat: Lives offshore south of Cape Hatteras to depths of about 100 feet. Occasionally washed onto ocean beaches.
Range: North Carolina to Texas and Brazil.
Notes: Members of this family are parasites, living on echinoderms such as sea stars, sea urchins, sand dollars and sea cucumbers. The animal has no radula but does have jaws that pierce the echinoderm's skin, allowing the mollusk to extend its mouth into its host. This species is often found in stomach of the sea star, *Astropecten articulatus.*

conoidal eulima

• **conoidal eulima** *Melanella conoidea* Kurtz & Stimpson (= *Balcis conoidea*)
Description: (3/8 inch) Acutely cone-shaped, glossy shell with flat-sided whorls. Angular shoulder and a slightly convex base on body whorl. Finely incised sutures. Elliptical aperture less than one-fourth the total shell length. No umbilicus.
Color: White to gray, sometimes with some brown.
Habitat: Lives offshore south of Cape Hatteras to depths of about 100 feet. Also lives in high-salinity estuaries such as Back and Bogue sounds near Beaufort Inlet. Occasionally washed onto ocean beaches.
Range: Cape Hatteras, N.C., to Florida and West Indies.
Notes: Also called a **cone-like balcis**. This species is sometimes hard to pick up because its surface is slick. Parasitic on sea cucumbers, *Holothuria* species. It feeds by sucking blood from the oral or anal end of the host. Often, this species is found in stomach of the sea star, *Astropecten articulatus*.

intermediate balcis

eastern mudsnail

* • **intermediate balcis** *Melanella intermedia* (Cantraine) (= *Balcis intermedia*)
Description: (1/2 inch) Similar to **conoidal eulima** except the shoulder of the body whorl is rounded instead of angular.
Color: Same as **conoidal eulima**.
Habitat: Same as **conoidal eulima**.
Range: New Jersey to Brazil.
Notes: Parasitic on the sea cucumber, *Holothuria impatiens*. See **conoidal eulima** ***Notes*** for feeding technique.

MUDSNAIL-SHAPED – mudsnails (Nassariidae)

• **eastern mudsnail** *Ilyanassa obsoleta* (Say)
(= *Nassarius obsoletus*)
Description: (1/2 inch) Small shell with a slightly rough surface. Weak spiral and axial ribs. Lower canal on oval aperture. Smooth inner lip with a parietal shield. Outer lip thin and smooth.
Color: Chalky white exterior, covered by a dark brown periostracum. Solid blackish brown parietal shield.
Habitat: Lives in intertidal zones of sounds and inlets. Common on sound and ocean beaches.
Range: Canada to Florida.
Notes: Also known as the **eastern mud nassa, mud dog whelk, mud basket shell** or **common mudsnail**. Often lives in large groups and helps keep mud flats clean by consuming decaying flesh. An omnivore, it is commonly considered a scavenger because it is quickly attracted to the odor of dead animals, but this species also eats microscopic plants and sometimes live animals. It has a specialized rod to aid in digestion. Females lay rows of funnel-shaped egg capsules with zigzagged ridges on seaweed, shells or rocks. Young are free-swimming.

bruised nassa

• **bruised nassa** *Nassarius vibex* (Say)
Description: (1/2 inch) Small shell with rough surface. Equal spiral and axial ribs, resulting in about 12 ridges and a coarsely beaded surface. Flattened whorls. Elongate aperture with canal at both ends. Smooth inner lip with prominent parietal shield. Thick and toothed outer lip.
Color: Grayish brown exterior, sometimes with brown bands or mottling. Prominent cream-colored parietal shield.
Habitat: Very common on shallow-water sand flats, in sounds, inlets and just offshore. Frequently found on sound and ocean beaches.
Range: Massachusetts to Brazil.
Notes: Also called a **common eastern nassa, mottled dog whelk** or **bruised basket shell**. A scavenger, it also has been observed feeding on eggs of marine worms. Females lay thin, oval egg capsules on seaweed, shells and rocks. Young are free-swimming.

threeline mudsnail

• **threeline mudsnail** *Ilyanassa trivattata* (Say)
(= *Nassarius trivattatus*)
Description: (3/4 inch) Small shell with rough surface. Spiral lines as strong as axial ribbing, resulting in beaded whorls. Shouldered whorls. Oval-shaped aperture with a canal at both ends. Smooth inner lip and scalloped outer lip. Small parietal shield. Thinner shell and higher spire than in other nassas.
Color: Exterior whitish to yellowish gray, sometimes with brownish bands.
Habitat: Occasionally washed onto ocean beaches or netted as incidental catch by offshore fishing boats.
Range: Nova Scotia, Canada, to Florida.
Notes: Also called a **New England nassa**, **New England dog whelk** or **New England basket shell**. A scavenger, it may also feed on moonsnail eggs. Young are free-swimming.

white nassa

• **white nassa** *Nassarius albus* (Say)
Description: (1/2 inch) Small shell with rough surface. Strong, rounded axial ribs crossed by many weaker spiral lines. Round aperture with a canal at both ends. Thick outer lip. Parietal shield not well-developed.
Color: White to yellowish exterior, sometimes with light brown spiral lines. White parietal shield.
Habitat: Lives offshore.
Range: North Carolina to Brazil.
Notes: Also called a **variable nassa**, **variable dog whelk** or **white basket shell**. This species is a scavenger. Young are free-swimming.

sharp nassa

• **sharp nassa** *Nassarius acutus* (Say)
Description: (1/2 inch) Small conical shell with a moderately high spire (slightly more than half the total shell length). Many axial ribs crossed by two spiral cords on whorls making up the spire. Sharp knob created by intersection of the axial and spiral ribs. Inner aperture lip usually thick and crenulated. Short, open front canal and sometimes a back canal on aperture. Lacks the enameled parietal shield on most nassas.
Color: Exterior white to creamish. On fresh specimens, a brown spiral thread may connect the knobs.
Habitat: Known living in intertidal areas of the Cape Fear area. Occasionally found on ocean beaches.
Range: North Carolina to Florida and Texas.
Notes: Also called a **sharp-knobbed nassa**, **sharp-knobbed dog whelk** or **narrow basket shell**. A scavenger, it is reported to feed on mollusk egg capsules.

MUDSNAIL-SHAPED – dovesnails (Columbellidae)

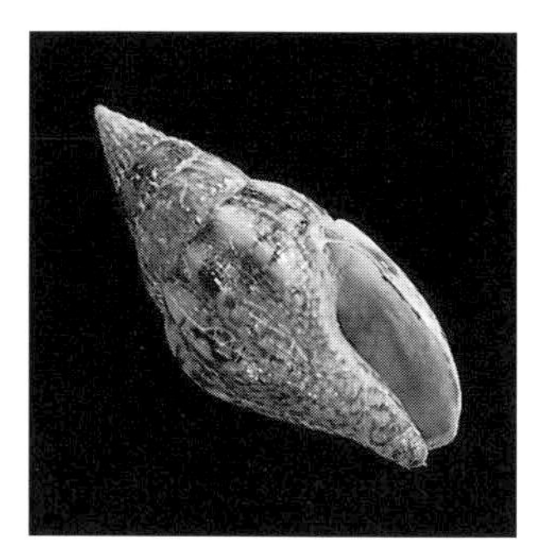

greedy dovesnail

• **greedy dovesnail** *Anachis avara* (Say) (= *Costoanachis avara*)
Description: (1/2 inch) Tiny, spindle-shaped shell with rough surface. Convex whorls. About 12 smooth axial ribs on top half of body whorl. No axial ribs on one or more earlier whorls. Spire longer than aperture. Elongate aperture with open lower canal. Outer lip weakly toothed. Small operculum.
Color: Gray to brownish yellow with whitish dots.
Habitat: Common on shallow-water sand flats in sounds, inlets and just offshore. Occasionally found on sound and ocean beaches.
Range: New Jersey to Brazil.
Notes: This species is probably a carnivore or scavenger. Females lay pyramid-shaped eggs on seaweed. Young are free-swimming.

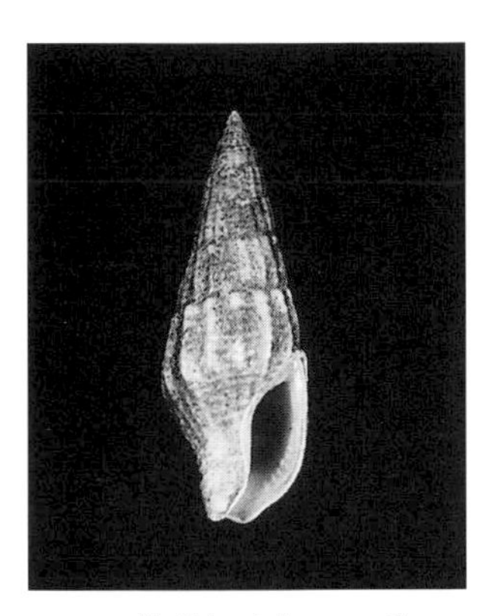

well-ribbed dovesnail

• **well-ribbed dovesnail** *Anachis lafresnayi* (P. Fischer & Bernardi) (= *Costoanachis lafresnayi, Anachis translirata* Raveneli)
Description: (1/2 inch) Similar to the **greedy dovesnail** except flat instead of convex whorls, a taller spire and stronger, more numerous (15 to 20) axial ribs that are noticeably crossed by spiral cords. Aperture less than half the total shell length.
Color: Gray to brownish yellow.
Habitat: Lives in near-offshore waters. Found washed onto sound and ocean beaches.
Range: Maine to Texas and Yucatan.
Notes: This species is a carnivore. Female lays volcano-shaped egg capsules on hard surfaces. Young are free-swimming.

lunar dovesnail

• **lunar dovesnail** *Mitrella lunata* (Say) (= *Astyris lunata*)
Description: (1/8 inch) Very small, oval shell (elongate yet plump) with a sharp spire. Flat-sided spire about equal in length to the aperture. Smooth whorls except for spiral lines on the body whorl base. Small, pointed and translucent early whorls. Elliptical aperture with a short canal at one end. Four small ridges on outer lip.
Color: Shiny cream to gray with many brown or reddish brown, zigzag axial stripes on each whorl.
Habitat: Lives in the intertidal zone, just offshore and sometimes in high-salinity estuaries. Often found crawling over seaweed, shell and sand. Commonly found on sound and ocean beaches.
Range: Massachusetts to Florida, Texas and Brazil.
Notes: A carnivore, it preys on small invertebrates attached to the bottom.

Florida dovesnail

• **Florida dovesnail** *Anachis floridana* Rehder (= *Costoanachis floridana*)
Description: (1/2 inch) Almost identical to the **greedy dovesnail**, it differs primarily by having axial ribbing only on the body whorl (no axial ribbing on the early whorls).
Color: Similar to **greedy dovesnail**.
Habitat: Known in Beaufort Inlet and nearby at 5- to 6-foot depths in the mouth of the Newport River.
Range: North Carolina to Florida and Texas.
Notes: Also called a **Florida dove shell**.

MUDSNAIL-SHAPED – nutmegs (Cancellariidae)

common nutmeg

* • **common nutmeg** *Cancellaria reticulata* (Linnaeus)
Description: (2 1/4 inches) Rough surface on shell. Many spiral cords across many axial ribs, resulting in a lattice or beaded pattern. Elongate aperture with short canal. Inner margin with two strong, thin spiral ridges running into aperture (upper ridge stronger than lower ridge). No operculum.
Color: Banded or splotched with cream and orange or brown.
Habitat: Lives offshore. Occasionally washed onto ocean beaches.
Range: North Carolina to Brazil.
Notes: This species is probably carnivorous because its radula is ideal for feeding on soft-bodied animals.

Smith nutmeg

* **Smith nutmeg** *Axelella smithii* (Dall) (= *Agatrix, Olssonella* or *Trigonostoma smithii*)
Description: (1/2 inch) Small shell with rough surface (axial ribs and spaces between them rough). Seven to nine strong, rounded axial ribs crossed by smaller spiral ridges. No extra large axial ribs. Oval aperture with open lower canal. Inner lip with spiral ridges running into aperture. Outer lip with cords running into aperture. No operculum.
Color: Brown to brownish red.
Habitat: Lives offshore, recorded to about 300-foot depths. Often netted as incidental catch in **Atlantic calico scallop** catches.
Range: North Carolina to South Carolina.
Notes: See **common nutmeg** ***Notes***.

MUDSNAIL-SHAPED – frogsnails (Bursidae)

chestnut frogsnail

• **chestnut frogsnail** *Bufonaria bufo* (Bruguière) (= *Bursa bufo, B. spadicea* Montfort)
Description: (2 1/4 inches) Shell's shape resembles a small frog. Rough surface with beaded spiral rows. Wide aperture with a deep canal at both ends. Inner lip with spiral ridges running into aperture. Appears flattened because the large, thick rib on left side is opposite the thick outer lip on right. Both lips toothed. Thin operculum.
Color: Dark brown and tan.
Habitat: Lives offshore. Occasionally found in **Atlantic calico scallop** catches.
Range: North Carolina to Brazil.
Notes: A carnivore, it is thought to anesthetize prey before digesting it. Females lay eggs in clusters on hard surfaces. Young are free-swimming.

MUDSNAIL-SHAPED – periwinkles (Littorinidae)

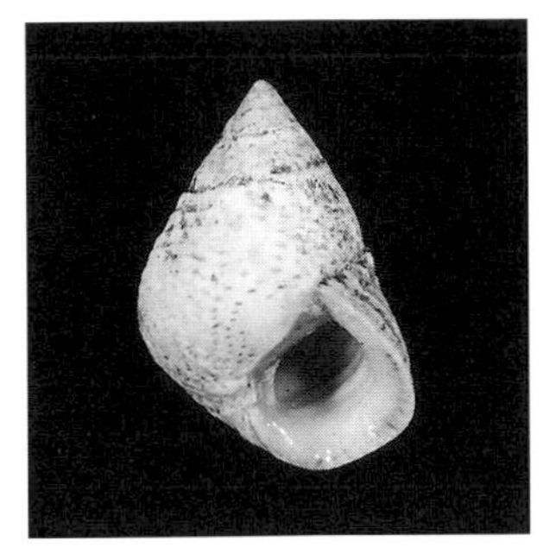

marsh periwinkle

• **marsh periwinkle** *Littorina irrorata* (Say)
Description: (1 inch) Small, top-shaped shell. Globelike body whorl and sharp spire. Spire less than twice the aperture length. Many regular spiral ridges. Round or elliptical aperture. Operculum.
Color: Grayish cream exterior with reddish streak on inner lip. Spiral cords often with dark, broken bands. Interior not iridescent.
Habitat: Lives in brackish marshes and on marsh grass. Frequently found on sound beaches.
Range: New York to Texas.
Notes: A herbivore, it scrapes algae from blades of marsh grass with its radula. Females lay floating egg capsules. Young are free-swimming.

MUDSNAIL-SHAPED – coli (Buccinidae)

Stimpson colus

* • **Stimpson colus** *Colus stimpsoni* (Morch)
Description: (4 1/2 inches) Spindle-shaped shell resembles a tulip shell. Rough exterior. Fragile shell. Fine spiral lines. Whorls not shouldered. Open upper canal on oval aperture. Tough periostracum.
Color: Chalky white exterior. White interior. Dark brown periostracum.
Habitat: Lives offshore, north of Cape Hatteras at depths greater than 900 feet. Generally found only on deep-water trawlers, particularly those fishing for lobster and **Atlantic deep-sea scallop**.
Range: Labrador, Canada, to North Carolina.
Notes: A carnivore and scavenger, it has radula that efficiently tear dead animal flesh.

tinted cantharus

• **tinted cantharus** *Pisania tincta* (Conrad) (= *Cantharus tinctus*)
Description: (1 1/4 inches) Spindle-shaped shell with rough surface. Surface sculpture of broad axial ribs and strong spiral ridges. Round aperture with a short canal at both ends. Smooth inner lip. Thick outer lip with many teeth.
Color: Exterior mottled brown, gray and cream. Interior white but occasionally with some brown blotches.
Habitat: Lives offshore. Occasionally found on rock jetties and ocean beaches.

Continued on next page

Continued from previous page

Range: North Carolina to Brazil.
Notes: Also called a **gaudy lesser whelk**. A carnivore, it feeds on small mollusks, worms and barnacles. See also **Florida rocksnail** ***Notes***.

ribbed cantharus

◊ • **ribbed cantharus** *Cantharus multangulus* (Philippi) (= *Pisania multangula*)
Description: (1 1/2 inches) Rough exterior. Axial ribs large and equal in size, but squarer than those on the **Caribbean coralsnail**. Spiral cords on ribs. Angular whorl shoulders. Wide aperture, about half the total length of the shell, ends in a short lower canal. Smooth inner margin with a spiral rib near the base. Horny operculum.
Color: Cream-orange exterior, usually with some brownish specks.
Habitat: Lives offshore.
Range: North Carolina to West Indies.
Notes: Also called a **false drill**. A carnivore, it probably feeds on small mollusks and barnacles below the low tide line. Females lay funnel-shaped egg capsules with spiny ridges around the top. Hatched young crawl away.

MUDSNAIL-SHAPED – coralsnails (Coralliophilidae)

Caribbean coralsnail

• **Caribbean coralsnail** *Coralliophia caribaea* Abbott (= *C. plicata*)
Description: (1 inch) Rough exterior. Large axial ribs equal in size. Whorls with angular shoulders. Wide aperture, more than half the total length of shell, ends in a short, slitlike lower canal. Smooth inner margin. Pointed apex.
Color: Frosty or chalky white exterior. Interior sometimes violet. Reddish operculum.
Habitat: Lives offshore. Has been found associated with **Atlantic calico scallop** beds.
Range: North Carolina to Brazil.
Notes: Also called a **Caribbean coral shell**. This species may resemble a **ribbed cantharus**. It is probably a carnivore. Members of this family have no radula. They feed on the coral and sea fans that they live among. Females keep egg capsules inside their shells until free-swimming young emerge.

staircase coralsnail

• **staircase coralsnail** *Coralliophila scalariformis* (Lamarck) (? = *Babelomurex mansfieldi* (McGinty), *Latiaxis mansfieldi)*
Description: (1 1/8 inches) Robust shell varied in shape. Seven to nine axial ribs with sharp spines on whorl shoulders. All whorls with moderate to strong, raised, scaly concentric cords (particularly strong on body whorl). Fine axial lines on nuclear whorls. Aperture somewhat longer than spire length. Rough edge on outer aperture lip. Open umbilicus.
Color: Grayish white exterior (light brown if periostracum is present). Shiny white aperture. Yellowish operculum.
Habitat: Lives south of Cape Lookout in depths of 55 to 360 feet. Associated with coral formations. Collected by scuba divers near the shipwreck of *John D. Gill.*
Range: North Carolina to Florida and West Indies.
Notes: Also called a **pagoda coral shell**. See **Caribbean coralsnail** ***Notes*** for feeding method.

MUDSNAIL-SHAPED – miters (Costellariidae)

harlequin miter

◊ • **harlequin miter** *Vexillum histrio* (Reeve) (= *Pusia histrio* or *Pusia albocincta* (C.B. Adams))
Description: (5/8 inch) Stout, spindle-shaped shell. Spire and aperture about the same length. Many axial ribs extending more than halfway down the base of the body whorl. Concentric lines across axial ribs and spaces between ribs. Four folds on inner lip of aperture (upper fold the strongest).
Color: Chocolate brown with a narrow white spiral band covering part of the axial ribbing.
Habitat: Collected by scuba divers on sandy bottom with **lions-paw scallops** at 100-foot depth off Wrightsville Beach.
Range: North Carolina, Florida to West Indies.
Notes: Also called a **painted miter**, **sulcate miter** or **white-lined miter.** This species may be confused in North Carolina waters with the **gem miter**, *Vexillum gemmatum* (Sowerby) (= *V. hanleyi* (Dohrn)), which has been found in similar areas and deeper waters off Beaufort Inlet. The **gem miter** is smaller, with a spire slightly longer than half the total shell length and several noduled ribs in a slightly concave area between the whorl suture and the axial ribbing below the suture.

OLIVE-SHAPED – olives (Olividae)

lettered olive

◊ • **lettered olive** *Oliva sayana* Ravenel
Description: (2 1/2 inches) Smooth, shiny, cylindrical shell with a short spire. Narrow aperture extending almost length of shell, continuing around the bottom and ending in a notch on the other side. Suture V-cut and deep. Lower part of whorl just above the suture extends outward and then at a sharp shoulder drops into the suture. No operculum.
Color: Cream or grayish exterior with reddish brown zigzag markings.
Habitat: Lives in near-shore waters on shallow sand flats near inlets. Occasionally to commonly washed onto ocean beaches.
Range: North Carolina to Gulf states.
Notes: This species is named for its dark surface markings that resemble letters. A carnivore, it captures bivalves and small crustaceans with its foot and takes them below the sand surface to digest. Its presence is sometimes detected at very low tides by the trails it leaves when it crawls below the surface on semi-exposed sand flats. Females lay floating, round egg capsules that are often found in beach drift. Young are free-swimming. Colonists and early Native Americans made jewelry from these shells.

brown olive

* • **brown olive** *Oliva reticularis bifasciata* Kuster
Description: (2 1/2 inches) Very similar to the **lettered olive** except this species in North Carolina waters has (1) a less pointed spire, (2) a channel suture not deeply V-cut and (3) a lower whorl portion that runs almost directly into the connecting suture. Also compare suture lines (see ***Color***).
Color: Similar to **lettered olive** except in this shell (1) the pattern is lighter and more reticulated than zigzag, (2) the color is yellowish and (3) brown spots that run from the suture "thread" or "bleed" down the shell (in the **lettered olive**, they do not).
Habitat: Lives in deep offshore waters. Found by divers near shipwrecks. Collected on sandy bottom near **lions-paw scallops** at 100-foot depth off Wrightsville Beach. From Wrightsville Beach to just above Cape Lookout, seems restricted to the edge of the continental shelf at about 300-foot depths.
Range: Cape Lookout, N.C., to West Indies.

variable dwarf olive

• variable dwarf olive *Olivella mutica* (Say)
Description: (1/2 inch) Small, smooth, shiny, olive-shaped shell. Spire almost half the total shell length. Narrow, triangular aperture with a narrow upper canal and a wider lower canal. Inner aperture wall with a thickened callus that extends almost to the suture of the previous whorl. No operculum.
Color: Creamy white exterior with about three deep reddish brown spiral bands. Occasionally solid brown.
Habitat: Lives on the sandy bottoms of sounds, inlets and offshore areas. Common on sound and ocean beaches.
Range: North Carolina to Bahamas.
Notes: This species is a carnivore. Females lay dome-shaped egg capsules on hard surfaces. Hatched young crawl away. It is closely related to the **lettered olive**. Of the six possible Olivellas off the North Carolina coast, this species may be the most common and easiest to identify.

OLIVE-SHAPED - cones (Conidae)

Floridensis cone

◊ * • **Floridensis cone** *Conus floridensis floridensis* Sowerby
Description: (1 1/2 inches) Smooth, shiny, cone-shaped shell. Fairly large spire with flat whorls. Narrow aperture almost the length of the shell.
Color: Yellowish background. Orange to yellowish brown spiral band and crowded dots. Body whorl may have one whitish spiral band.
Habitat: Lives offshore among **Atlantic calico scallop** beds. Rarely washed onto ocean beaches.
Range: North Carolina to Florida.
Notes: Resembles **Sozon cone** except it is smaller and has different markings. Live cones should always be handled with care. Pacific Ocean species are known to inflict a semipoisonous sting; Atlantic Ocean species are not believed to have a dangerous sting. A carnivore, it searches for prey at night, mainly at low tide. Females lay eggs in rows of flat capsules on hard surfaces or underneath rocks. Young are free-swimming.

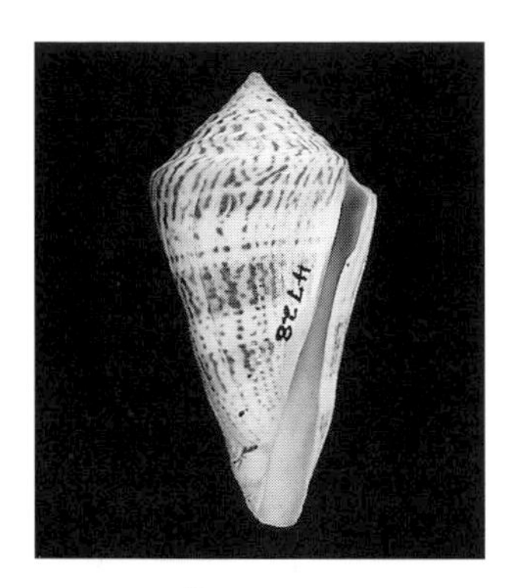
Sozon cone

◊ * • **Sozon cone** *Conus delessertii* Recluz (= *C. sozoni* Bartsch)
Description: (4 inches) Smooth, shiny, cone-shaped shell with a well-developed spire. Narrow aperture almost the length of the shell. Resembles the **Floridensis cone** but larger with different markings (see ***Color***).
Color: Yellow-orange with two large white spiral bands. Many rows of irregular brown lines and spots encircle the shell.
Habitat: Lives offshore. Rarely found on ocean beaches.
Range: North Carolina to Florida.
Notes: See **Floridensis cone** ***Notes***. This species was commonly brought in with **Atlantic calico scallop** catches.

Julia cone

* • **Julia cone** *Conus amphiurgus juliae* Clench
Description: (2 inches) Smooth, shiny, cone-shaped shell with a fairly high spire. Sides of whorls flattened. Body whorl sculptured by finely incised spiral lines and irregular growth lines. Slightly rounded shoulders. Narrow aperture almost length of shell.
Color: Body whorl a light pinkish brown to orange with a creamy white spiral band at the middle. Middle band interrupted with axial bars of the body color, making it appear flecked with brown or broken spiral lines. Whitish spire with red streaks on the shoulder.
Habitat: Lives in deep offshore waters in rubble and sand. Collected by scuba divers on sandy bottom at 100-foot depths.
Range: South of Cape Lookout, N.C., to Texas and West Indies.
Notes: This species is rare. It is usually found by divers.

dusky cone

• **dusky cone** *Conus stearnsi* Conrad
Description: (3/4 inch) Small, cone-shaped shell with a high spire that makes up about one-third the shell length. Sides of the spire form a 70-degree angle. Shoulders of early whorls concave with flat sides, making spire slightly concave. Body whorl sculptured with about 13 incised spiral lines.
Color: Gray body whorl; brownish dots on incised spiral lines.
Habitat: Collected by scuba divers on sandy bottom at 65-foot depths.
Range: South of Cape Lookout, N.C., to Florida and Yucatan.

OLIVE-SHAPED – marginellas (Marginellidae)

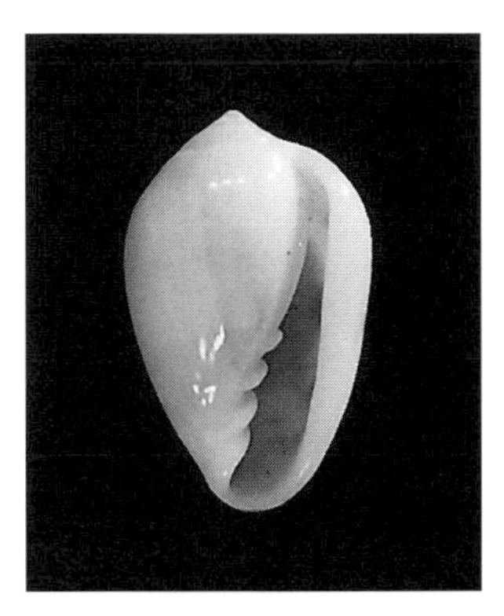

common Atlantic marginella

• **common Atlantic marginella** *Marginella apicina* Menke (= *Prunum apicinum*)
Description: (1/2 inch) Tiny, glossy, cone-shaped shell with a tiny spire. Narrow aperture almost the length of the shell. Four folds on inner lip. Similar to **seaboard marginella** except wider, lacks white specks and teeth on the thickened outer lip. No operculum.
Color: Golden brown exterior, usually with two to three darker spiral bands. White outer lip with two to four brownish spots. Living specimens considerably lighter than living specimens of the **seaboard marginella**.
Habitat: Lives near inlets and offshore.
Range: North Carolina to Brazil. Author believes many earlier published North Carolina records of this species are in error and should be of the **seaboard marginella**.
Notes: Also called an **Atlantic margin shell**. A carnivore, it moves quickly over the sand in search of food. Females lay dome-shaped, pimpled egg capsules. Hatched young crawl away. Early Native Americans often crafted necklaces from margin shells and used them in trading.

seaboard marginella

◊ • **seaboard marginella** *Marginella roscida* Redfield (= *Prunum roscidum*)
Description: (1/2 inch) Tiny, glossy, cone-shaped shell with a tiny spire. Very narrow aperture almost the length of shell. Four folds on inner lip. Similar to **common Atlantic marginella** but narrower, with white specks and teeth on the thickened outer aperture lip. No operculum.
Color: Cream exterior with three brownish spiral bands and covering of white flecks. Outer lip with four brown spots.
Habitat: Lives near inlets and offshore. Occasionally found on sound and ocean beaches.
Range: North Carolina to South Carolina.
Notes: Also called a **Jersey marginella**. See **common Atlantic marginella** *Notes*.

OLIVE-SHAPED – volutes (Volutidae)

junonia

◊ • **junonia** *Scaphella junonia* (Shaw)
Description: (5 1/4 inches) Spindle-shaped shell with a smooth, shiny surface and spectacular color. Moderate spire. Elongate aperture with short, open lower canal. Inner lip with folds and ridges. Smooth outer lip. No operculum.
Color: Cream background with large purple spots.
Habitat: Lives offshore in colonies on ocean floor. Rarely washed up after storms on ocean beaches. Sometimes brought in on shrimp boats.
Range: North Carolina to Texas.
Notes: A carnivore, it feeds on small invertebrates. This species is prized by collectors. It is named for spots on the shell and mantle, which reminded people in earlier times of the tail of a peacock, the "bird of Juno."

OLIVE-SHAPED – melampi (Melampodidae)

eastern melampus

• **eastern melampus** *Melampus bidentatus* Say
Description: (5/8 inch) Small, cone-shaped shell with a short, blunt spire. Sides of the spire form a 90-degree angle. Fine spiral lines on spire and body whorl. Long, narrow aperture with front end expanded. About nine spiral ridges on outer lip; two to three folds on inner lip.
Color: Light to dark brown, occasionally with three to four darker-colored spiral bands.
Habitat: Lives in the high tide zone of salt marshes in moderate- to high-salinity estuaries. Typically found under boards or marsh grass (*Spartina*) litter or at the base of *Spartina* stalks. Occasionally found on some sound beaches.
Range: Nova Scotia, Canada, to Texas and West Indies.
Notes: Also called a **salt-marsh snail**. This family has a primitive lung in place of gills and breathes air. The snail eats decaying plant matter but is believed to get its nutrients from the bacteria that live on decaying matter. Female lays eggs in jellylike mounds, each containing about 840 eggs. Larvae settle to the bottom during autumn's spring tides (high tides during full and new moons).

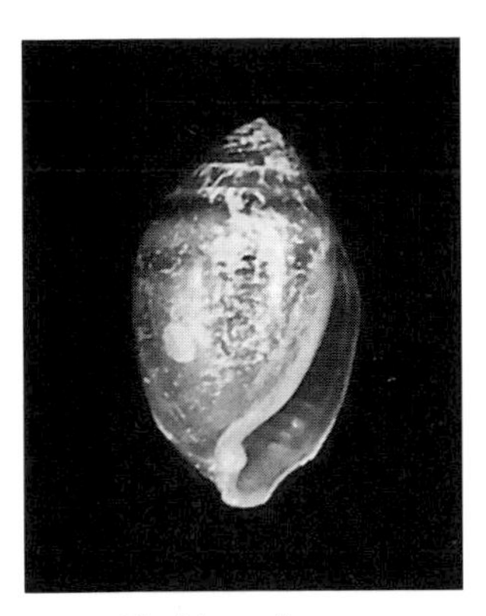

Florida melampus

• **Florida melampus** *Detracia floridana* (Pfeiffer)
Description: (less than 1/4 inch) Similar to the **eastern melampus** except smaller with a higher spire and no incised spiral lines on the shoulder. About 10 spiral ridges on outer lip. One large and one small tooth or ridge on inner lip.
Color: Glossy dark brown with several light brown spiral bands on the body whorl.
Habitat: Lives on or under marsh debris in the high tide zone of low-salinity marshes, sometimes alongside the **eastern melampus**.
Range: New Jersey to Louisiana.
Notes: Many of this species may be found living in a restricted area. Like the **eastern melampus**, it breathes air with primitive lungs. Its feeding habits also may be similar. Females lay 20 to 50 eggs in domelike, gelatinous masses. Free-swimming larvae hatch in about two weeks. Crabs, fish and birds prey on the adults.

OLIVE-SHAPED – cowries (Cypraeidae)

Atlantic deer cowrie

◊ • **Atlantic deer cowrie** *Cypraea cervus* Linnaeus
Description: (6 inches) Glossy, smooth, thin, elongate shell with no spire and a narrow aperture the length of the shell. Aperture lips curved and heavily ridged (resembling a mouth with teeth). Large canal-like depression at both ends. No operculum.
Color: Light to dark brown with many white spots. Color pattern similar to that of a young fawn. Dark brown aperture teeth.
Habitat: Lives offshore on rocks and shipwrecks south of Cape Hatteras. Rarely washed onto ocean beaches.
Range: North Carolina to Yucatan.
Notes: This species feeds at night, but its diet is unknown. Young havc brown spiral bands the spots and aperture teeth appear as the animals mature. Females lay egg capsules in crevices and protect them with their foot. Young are free-swimming. Early Native Americans used cowries as money in trading. Many cultures used cowries as religious and fertility symbols.

Atlantic yellow cowrie

• **Atlantic yellow cowrie** *Cypraea spurca acicularis* Gmelin
Description: (3/4 inch) Tiny, glossy, elongate shell with no spire and a narrow aperture the length of the shell. Similar in shape to the **Atlantic deer cowrie** but smaller and flatter. Heavily ridged aperture lips (resembling teeth). Large canal-like depression at both ends of aperture. No operculum.
Color: Yellowish-tan exterior with small yellowish spots. Whitish aperture teeth.
Habitat: Lives offshore.
Range: North Carolina to Brazil.
Notes: See **Atlantic deer cowrie** *Notes*.

OLIVE-SHAPED – trivias (Triviidae)

coffeebean trivia

• **coffeebean trivia** *Trivia pediculus* (Linnaeus)
Description: (1/2 inch) Small, globe-shaped shell flattened above, with 16 to 18 cords circling the shell. Small groove down back of the shell. Narrow, toothed aperture extending the length of the shell. Ornate mantle almost completely covers the shell.
Color: Light brown or pinkish brown with three dark brown patches on the back.
Habitat: Lives in deep offshore waters on shipwrecks. Found by scuba divers south of Cape Lookout at 50-foot depths.
Range: North Carolina to Brazil.
Notes: It resembles a cowrie shell, but the animal inside is different. A carnivore, it feeds on tunicates. Females deposit egg capsules inside the flesh of tunicates. Young are free-swimming. The attractive shell is often used in jewelry.

OLIVE-SHAPED – simnias & cyphomas (Ovulidae)

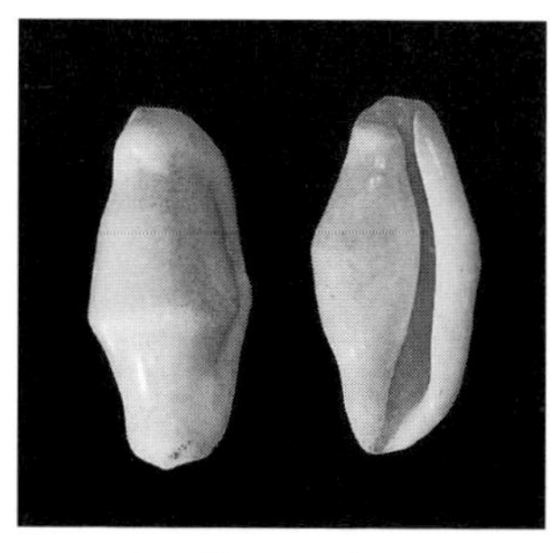
McGinty cyphoma

* • **McGinty cyphoma** *Cyphoma mcgintyi* Pilsbry
Description: (1 1/4 inches) Smooth, glossy, elongate shell resembling a pair of lips with no teeth (both lips of the long, narrow aperture are smooth). Humped back with one swollen ridge. No spire. When alive, mantle may completely cover the shell. No operculum.
Color: Cream-colored shell. Cream-colored mantle with dark brown spots and occasionally a pink or lavender tint. When alive, vivid patterns on shell and mantle.

Continued on upper right

Continued from lower left

Habitat: Lives south of Cape Hatteras on sea fans and sea whips in inlets and offshore. Rarely found on beaches.
Range: North Carolina to Florida.
Notes: Also known as **McGinty's flamingo tongue**. A carnivore, it lives and feeds on sea fans and whips. Males are territorial and defend certain portions of an individual sea fan. Females lay clumps of eggs on the branches. Young are free-swimming. This species is used in jewelry.

one-tooth simnia

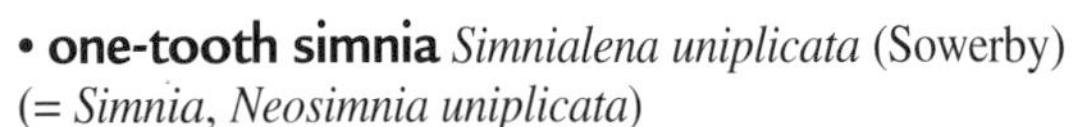

• **one-tooth simnia** *Simnialena uniplicata* (Sowerby) (= *Simnia, Neosimnia uniplicata*)
Description: (3/4 inch) Small, thin, almost cylindrical shell. Smooth, glossy exterior. No spire. Very narrow aperture almost the length of the shell. Open canals at both ends of aperture. Both lips smooth. Several folds on lower part of inner aperture wall. Slightly thickened outer lip.
Color: Exterior yellow, orange or occasionally light purple. Network of brown lines on mantle.
Habitat: Lives in inlets and offshore on living sea whips. Rarely found on beaches.
Range: Virginia to Brazil.
Notes: This species is a carnivore. The shell and mantle color depend on the color of the sea whips it feeds on. Males defend territories on sea whips. Females lay eggs on the branches. Young are free-swimming.

OLIVE-SHAPED – bubbles (Bullidae)

striate bubble

• **striate bubble** *Bulla striata* Brugière (= *B. occidentalis* A. Adams)
Description: (1 3/4 inches) Smooth, shiny, oval shell. Looks as though rolled up or folded over. Depressed spire; hole in apex where the spire should be. Aperture extends length of the shell, narrow above and much wider and rounded below. No operculum.
Color: Mottled exterior with light and dark brown.
Habitat: Occasionally found washed onto ocean beaches.
Range: North Carolina to Brazil.
Notes: Also called a **common Atlantic bubble**. An omnivore, it feeds on other mollusks and algae at night. It burrows just below sand surface during the day. This species is a hermaphrodite.

OLIVE-SHAPED – barrel-bubbles (Scaphandridae)

Candé barrel-bubble

* • **Candé barrel-bubble** *Acteocina candei* (d'Orbigny)
Description: (less than 1/4 inch) Very small, smooth, glossy shell. Barrel- to spindle-shaped with straightish sides. Short spire with early whorls at 90-degree angle to later whorls (heterostropic condition). Spiral carina on the shoulder suture. Narrow aperture almost the length of shell until it widens out at the front end. Inner lip with a thickened fold.
Color: Milky white.
Habitat: Lives in high-salinity estuaries and just offshore. Found in beach drift south of Cape Hatteras.
Range: North Carolina to Argentina.
Notes: Larvae are free-swimming.

channeled barrel-bubble

• **channeled barrel-bubble** *Acteocina canaliculata* (Say)
Description: (less than 1/4 inch) Similar to **Candé barrel-bubble** except early whorls almost completely submerged in the spire; shoulder suture slightly channeled and without a spiral carina.
Color: White to cream with rustlike staining.
Habitat: Lives in estuarine waters. Found in beach drift.
Range: Nova Scotia, Canada, to Florida, Texas and West Indies.
Notes: Females lay eggs in a round jellylike mass that is attached by a stalk to the sand or mud. Larvae either develop immediately into crawling young or pass through a short free-swimming stage.

HELMET-SHAPED – helmet (Cassidae)

Scotch bonnet

• **Scotch bonnet** *Phalium granulatum* (Born)
Description: (3 1/2 inches) Globelike shell with short spire and many smooth to occasionally barred spiral ridges. Light axial cords near shoulder. Occasionally, thickened rib indicates remains of earlier thick outer lip. Wide aperture with canals at both ends. Thick, toothed outer lip. Inner lip forms a parietal shield with raised pustules on lower part. Operculum.
Color: White exterior with some spiral rows of square, brownish orange spots.
Habitat: Lives offshore. Shell fragments common on ocean beaches after storms, but whole specimens found only occasionally.
Range: North Carolina to Uruguay.
Notes: This species was declared North Carolina's official seashell (by act of the N.C. General Assembly in May 1965 in memory of the state's early Scottish settlers). North Carolina

Continued on upper right

Continued from lower left

was the first state to designate an official seashell. A carnivore, it searches out and feeds on sea urchins and sand dollars; it secretes acid to digest them. Females lay eggs in round "towers" and sit on them. Young are free-swimming. A closely related but very rare offshore species, the **Coronado bonnet**, *Phalium coronadoi* (Crosse), grows to 3 1/2 inches in length, has several rows of low knobs near its shoulder and is a solid brownish tan. Note section on page 6, "Studying and Collecting Shells."

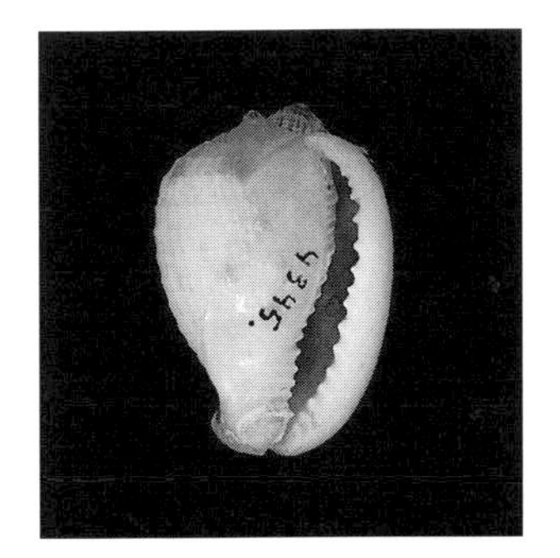

reticulate cowrie-helmet

◊ • **reticulate cowrie-helmet** *Cypraecassis testiculus* (Linnaeus)
Description: (2 3/4 inches) Inflated, helmetlike shell with a small spire. Narrow aperture almost the length of shell. Axial ribs crossed by spiral grooves, forming a reticulated surface. Smooth parietal shield. Small upper canal and deep, slitlike lower canal on aperture. Inner and outer aperture lips heavily ridged. No operculum in adults.
Color: Tan-orange exterior with spiral rows of dark brown spots. Orange to white parietal shield and outer lip. Row of dark brown spots also on outer lip.
Habitat: Lives offshore. Rarely washed onto ocean beaches.
Range: North Carolina to Brazil.
Notes: A carnivore, it feeds on sea urchins and sand dollars — see **Scotch bonnet** ***Notes***. Females lay eggs in tubelike clumps under stones and shells. Young are free-swimming.

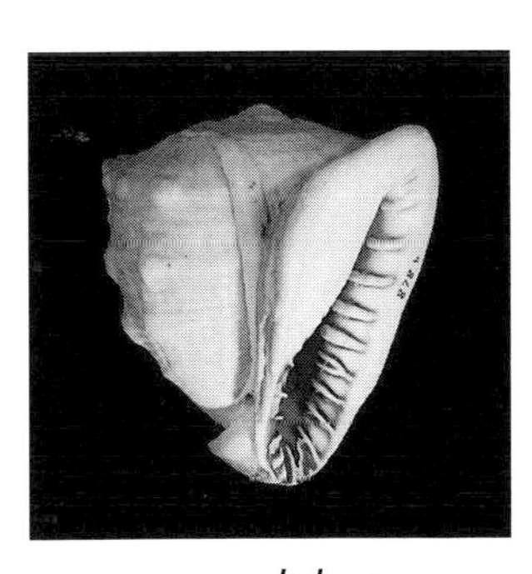

cameo helmet

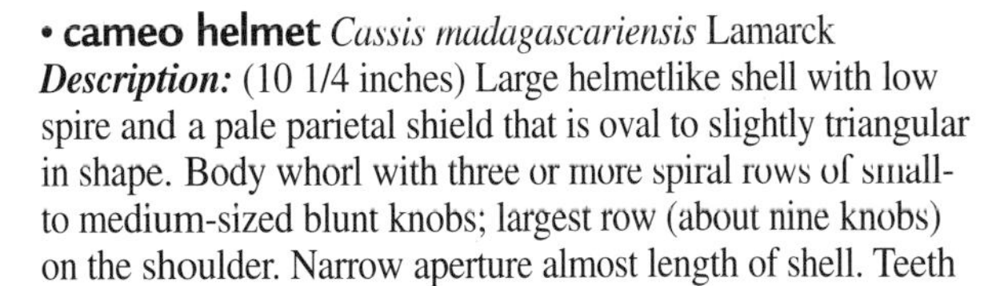

• **cameo helmet** *Cassis madagascariensis* Lamarck
Description: (10 1/4 inches) Large helmetlike shell with low spire and a pale parietal shield that is oval to slightly triangular in shape. Body whorl with three or more spiral rows of small- to medium-sized blunt knobs; largest row (about nine knobs) on the shoulder. Narrow aperture almost length of shell. Teeth on both lips. Small, narrow operculum.
Color: Body whorl exterior yellowish white with faint tan markings. Large pale brown or orange parietal shield. White aperture teeth with dark brown between them. Brown interior.
Habitat: Lives offshore, mainly off the Outer Banks near the Gulf Stream. At one time, whole shells common on Cape Lookout beaches. Now, only occasional pieces found on ocean beaches south of Cape Hatteras.
Range: North Carolina to West Indies.
Notes: Also called an **emperor helmet** or **queen helmet**. This species is one of the largest helmet shells in the world. A carnivore, it feeds on sea urchins and sand dollars — see **Scotch bonnet** ***Notes***. Young are free-swimming.

Clench helmet

* • **Clench helmet** *Cassis madagascariensis spinella* Clench
Description: (10 1/2 to 14 inches) Similar to **cameo helmet** but usually larger with about 12 small knobs on the shoulder of the body whorl; one or two additional spiral rows of smaller knobs sometimes below shoulder.
Color: Similar to **cameo helmet** except sometimes lighter.
Habitat: Lives offshore on sandy or shelly bottoms to depths of about 120 feet. Frequently brought up by scuba divers and fishing trawlers from **Atlantic calico scallop** beds.
Range: South of Cape Hatteras, N.C., to Florida.
Notes: This is a form of the **cameo helmet** (*Cassis madagascariensis*) found in North Carolina waters. It is one of the largest helmet shells in the world. A carnivore, it feeds on sea urchins and sand dollars — see **Scotch bonnet** ***Notes***. Young are free-swimming.

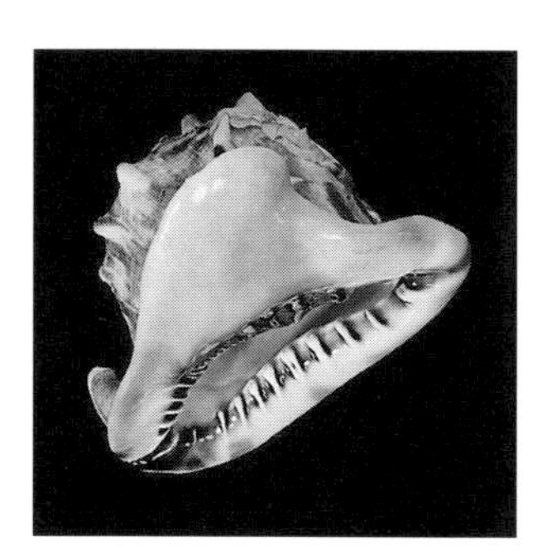

Caribbean helmet

◊ • **Caribbean helmet** *Cassis tuberosa* (Linnaeus)
Description: (9 inches) Similar to **cameo helmet** but smaller, with a more pointed triangular parietal shield.
Color: Similar to **cameo helmet** but with seven or eight dark brown zigzag or crescent-shaped markings. Squarish spots of reddish brown on outer aperture lip. Black between teeth.
Habitat: Lives offshore on sand and grass. Found by scuba divers at 200-foot depths off the North Carolina coast.
Range: North Carolina (rare) to Brazil.
Notes: Also known as the **king helmet**. This species is the most common south Atlantic helmet. A carnivore, it feeds on sea urchins — see **Scotch bonnet** ***Notes***. Young are free-swimming.

HELMET-SHAPED – tuns (Tonnidae)

giant tun

• **giant tun** *Tonna galea* (Linnaeus)
Description: (7 1/2 inches) Large, globe-shaped, fragile shell with a rough surface. Nineteen to 21 broad, flattened, widely spaced spiral ridges. Long spire. Large aperture. No operculum on adults. Slightly flared outer lip. Varnishlike periostracum.
Color: White to brown, sometimes streaked with brown. Tip of spire deep golden brown.
Habitat: Lives offshore. Rarely found on ocean beaches.
Range: North Carolina to Argentina.
Notes: A carnivore, it swallows animals whole and secretes acid to digest them. Females lay eggs in wide rows. Young are free-swimming.

MOONSNAIL-SHAPED – **moonsnail** (Naticidae)

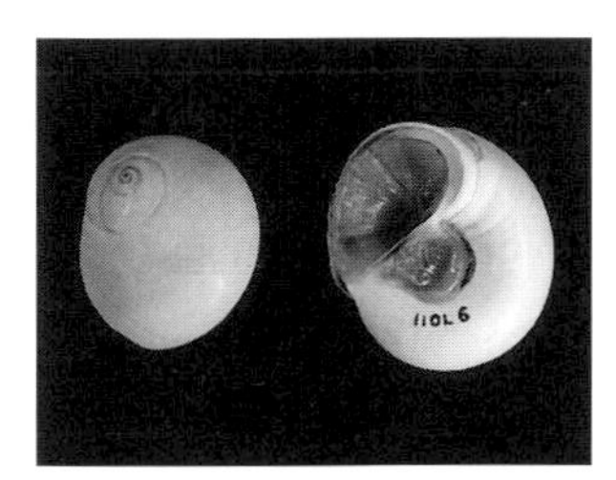

shark eye

• **shark eye** *Neverita duplicata* (Say) (= *Polinices duplicatus*)
Description: (3 1/2 inches) Smooth, globe-shaped shell with a small spire. Resembles a shark's eye because line winds around the spire. Umbilicus almost covered by a large, buttonlike lobe. Large elliptical aperture. Horny operculum.
Color: Bluish brown or purplish gray with a gray umbilicus, brown callus and a light brown semitransparent operculum.
Habitat: Lives offshore. Commonly washed onto sound and ocean beaches.
Range: Cape Cod, Mass., to Texas.
Notes: Also called an **Atlantic moonsnail**. A carnivore, it is a very active predator that burrows rapidly through sand to find prey. It attacks other mollusks, including relatives, by using its radula and acid secretions to drill a beveled hole through the prey's shell. This species leaves tracks over sand at low tide. Females lay eggs under "sand collars," which they form out of mucus and sand grains; these can often be found on beaches during the summer. Young are free-swimming.

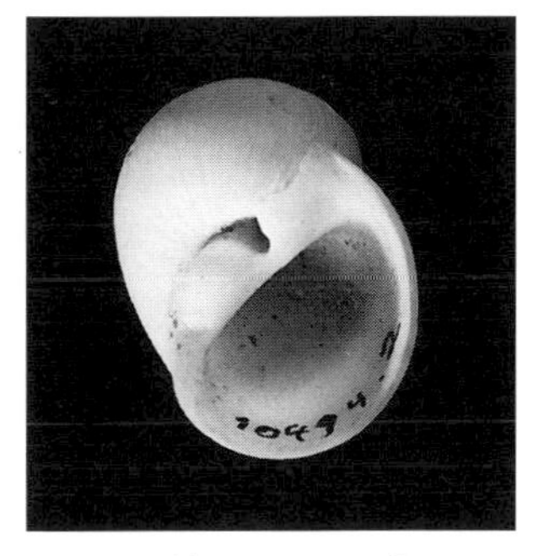

white moonsnail

• **white moonsnail** *Polinices uberinus* (d'Orbigny)
Description: (3/4 inch) Small, smooth, globe-shaped shell. No spiral cords on whorl. Umbilicus partially covered by a button-shaped lobe. Large elliptical aperture. Horny operculum.
Color: Glossy white exterior. White callus. Red operculum.
Habitat: Lives offshore. Has been found in **Atlantic calico scallop** beds.
Range: North Carolina to Florida.
Notes: Also called a **dwarf white moon shell**. See **shark eye** *Notes*.

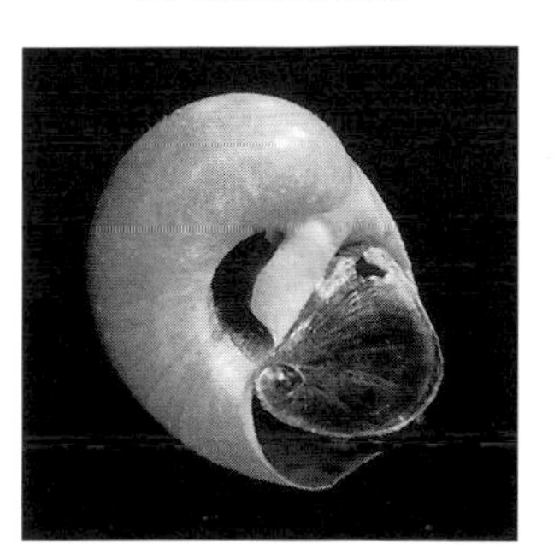

milk moonsnail

• **milk moonsnail** *Polinices lacteus* (Guilding)
Description: (3/4 inch) Solid, ovate, slightly oblong shell with a short spire. Deep, narrow umbilicus partially covered by a buttonlike callus. Oval aperture with a flattened inner lip. Horny operculum. Thin and smooth periostracum.
Color: Shiny, milky white exterior. Reddish brown operculum. Yellowish periostracum. Similar to **white moonsnail**.
Habitat: Lives in waters just off the southern North Carolina coast. Somewhat commonly found by scuba divers.
Range: North Carolina to Florida and Brazil.
Notes: See **shark eye** *Notes*. This species has a spiral sand collar.

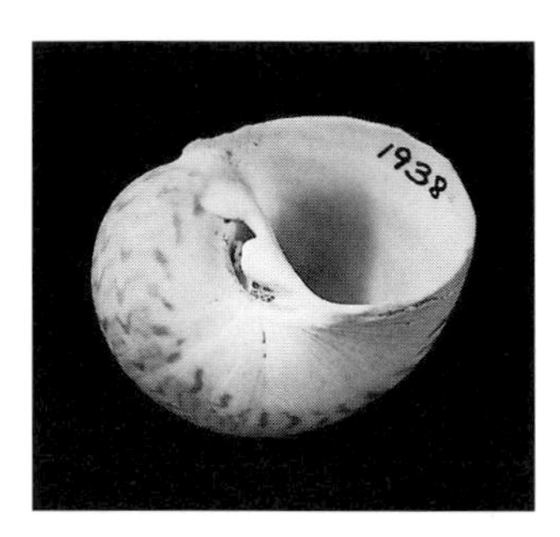

colorful moonsnail

• **colorful moonsnail** *Natica canrena* (Linnaeus)
Description: (1 3/4 inches) Smooth, globe-shaped shell with a small spire. Umbilicus area almost covered by a calcareous pad. Large and elliptical aperture. Calcareous operculum.
Color: Yellow-tan with broad tan or brown spiral bands crossed by narrow dark-brown axial zigzags or marks. White umbilicus, calcareous pad and operculum. Interior not iridescent.
Habitat: Lives offshore.
Range: North Carolina to Uruguay.
Notes: Also known as the **colorful Atlantic natica**. See **shark eye *Notes***.

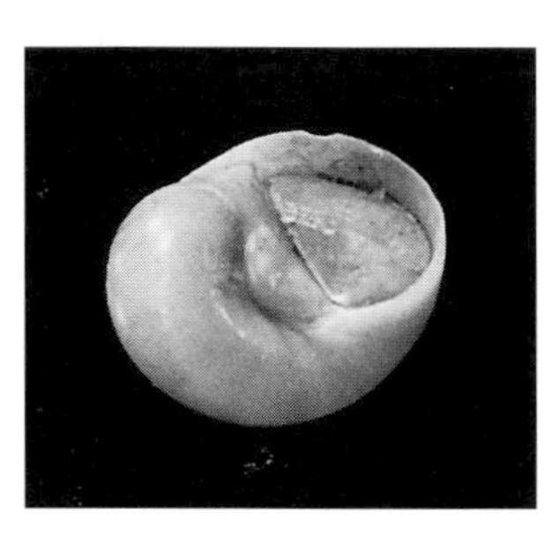

miniature moonsnail

• **miniature moonsnail** *Tectonatica pusilla* (Say) (= *Natica pusilla*)
Description: (1/4 inch) Small, stout, oval shell with a short spire. Narrow umbilicus almost covered by a callus. Oval aperture with flattened inner lip. Flattened calcareous operculum.
Color: Shiny tan exterior. Body whorl with a light brown mid-band of solid or irregular axial markings.
Habitat: Lives just offshore. Occasionally washed onto ocean beaches.
Range: Maine to Florida and Brazil.
Notes: Frequently found in stomach of the orange and blue sea star, *Astropecten articulatus*. See **shark eye *Notes*** for feeding habits.

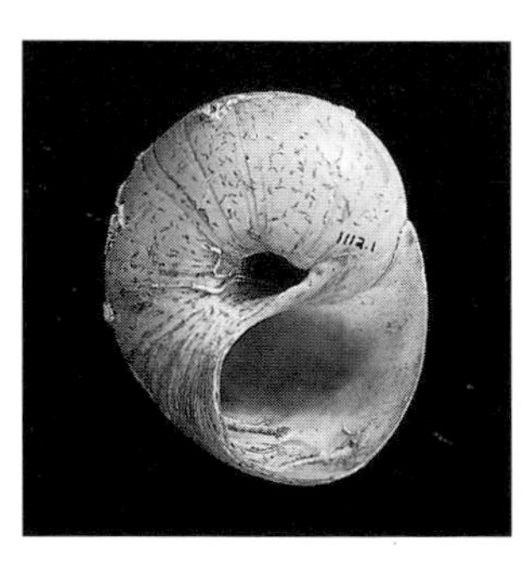

northern moonsnail

• **northern moonsnail** *Euspira heros* (Say) (= *Lunatia heros*)
Description: (4 1/4 inches) Smooth, globe-shaped shell. Small, deep umbilicus covered only slightly by a button-shaped lobe. Large elliptical aperture. Horny operculum.
Color: Bluish gray with gray umbilicus. Light brown operculum. Yellowish periostracum.
Habitat: Occasionally washed onto ocean beaches.
Range: Canada to Cape Hatteras, N.C.
Notes: See **shark eye *Notes***. Specimens found on beaches south of Cape Hatteras are probably fossil shells.

white baby-ear

• white baby-ear *Sinum perspectivum* (Say)
Description: (1 3/4 inches) Flat, smooth, ovate shell. Well-named. Low spiral cords on upper side of whorl. When alive, almost completely covered by mantle; resembles a piece of white gristle. No umbilicus. Large, round aperture. No operculum.
Color: White exterior. Pale brown periostracum. Yellowish cream mantle.
Habitat: Commonly found in shallow offshore waters and washed onto ocean beaches.
Range: Maryland to Brazil.
Notes: Also called a **common Atlantic baby-ear**. See **shark eye** *Notes*.

brown baby-ear

• brown baby-ear *Sinum maculatum* (Say)
Description: (1 3/4 inches) Similar to **white baby-ear** but not as flat (spire protrudes slightly). Low spiral cords on upper side of whorl. When alive, mantle almost completely surrounds shell. No umbilicus. Large, round aperture. No operculum.
Color: Light brown exterior. Mantle spotted with reddish brown.
Habitat: Lives offshore.
Range: North Carolina to Brazil.
Notes: Also called a **maculated baby-ear** or **spotted baby-ear**. See **shark eye** *Notes*.

MOONSNAIL-SHAPED – janthinas (Janthinidae)

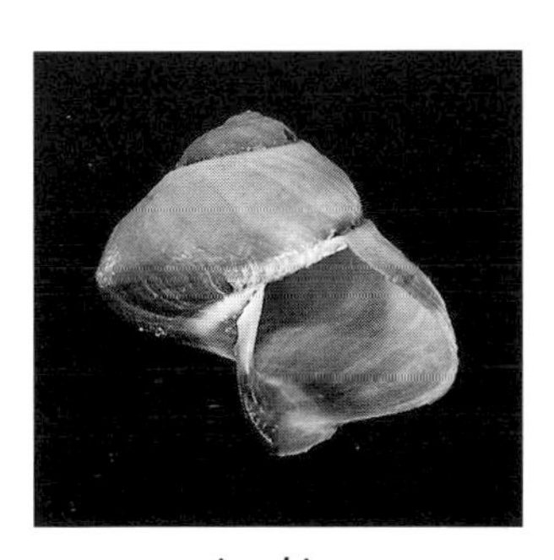

janthina

• janthina *Janthina janthina* (Linnaeus)
Description: (1 inch) Smooth, fragile shell with three or four sloping whorls that are rounded but slightly angular. Large aperture round or elliptical. Thin lip hangs below whorls. Inner margin of aperture extends downward, forming a rounded intersection with the outer lip. No umbilicus or operculum.
Color: Top half of shell light purple. Lower half deep purple. Interior not iridescent.
Habitat: Lives suspended upside down from a "raft" of bubbles on the ocean surface. Sometimes found washed onto beaches after storms.
Range: Warm Atlantic and Pacific waters.

Continued on next page

Continued from previous page

Notes: Also called a **common purple snail** or **violet snail**. This carnivore feeds on tiny jellyfish, *Velella* and *Physalia*, and is often found on these creatures. A hermaphrodite, the male stage occurs first. Young males mate with the older individuals that have transformed to females. Young are free-swimming. Adult life is spent in the open ocean, hanging upside down by its foot from a raft of bubbles. It forms the bubbles by trapping air inside mucus with its foot. Its dependence on the currents has resulted in the loss of its ability to move on its own.

elongate janthina

◊ • **elongate janthina** *Janthina globosa* Swainson
Description: (1 inch) Smooth, fragile shell with about three well-rounded whorls. Large, elliptical aperture. Thin angular lip hangs below whorls. Inner margin of aperture extends downward, forming an angular juncture with the outer lip. No umbilicus or operculum.
Color: Top and bottom halves nearly the same shade of violet. Iridescent interior.
Habitat: Lives suspended upside down from a raft of bubbles on the ocean surface. Occasionally found on ocean beaches after storms.
Range: Warm Atlantic and Pacific waters.
Notes: Also called a **globe violet snail**. See **janthina *Notes***.

TOP-SHAPED – keyhole limpets (Fissurellidae)

Cayenne keyhole limpet

• **Cayenne keyhole limpet** *Diodora cayenensis* (Lamarck)
Description: (1 inch) Shell shaped like a small, low cone or a coolie hat. Many ribs radiating from the small, subcentral keyholelike opening on top of shell. Inside of keyhole opening outlined by a truncate callus with a deep pit on its concave edge.
Color: Exterior white and pinkish gray or brown. Interior white to gray.
Habitat: Lives in inlets and offshore waters attached to rocks or shells. Occasionally found on sound and ocean beaches.
Range: New Jersey to Brazil.
Notes: Also called a **little keyhole limpet**. A herbivore, it uses radula to scrape algae off of rocks. Its powerful foot creates strong suction to keep waves from washing it off the rocks. Water enters under the edge of the shell and exits through the "keyhole" near the peak. Its eggs are yellow and stick to rocks. Hatched young crawl away.

TOP-SHAPED – turbans (Turbinidae)

chestnut turban

• **chestnut turban** *Turbo castanea* Gmelin
Description: (1 1/2 inches) Heavy, top-shaped shell resembling a turban. Rounded whorls. Outer surface rough, knobby and beaded. Rounded or elliptical aperture. Round, calcareous operculum.
Color: Exterior gray, brown or greenish with brown splotches. Interior iridescent and shiny. White operculum.
Habitat: Lives in inlets and offshore. Occasionally washed onto ocean beaches.
Range: North Carolina to Brazil.
Notes: Also called a **knobby turban**. This species is a herbivore. Females release eggs into the water. Young are free-swimming. It is related to a Pacific shell called a **cat's eye**.

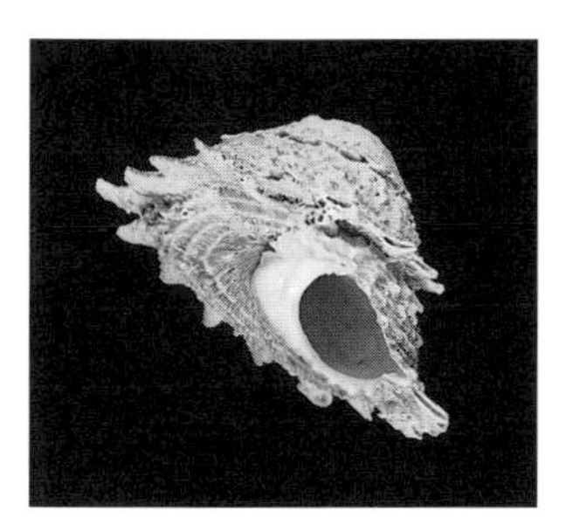

longspine starsnail

• **longspine starsnail** *Astralium phoebium* (Röding)
(= *Astraea phoebia*, *A. longispina* Lamarck)
Description: (2 inches wide, including spines) Heavy, top-shaped shell with triangular spines radiating from flat whorls, resembling the sun. Flat base of shell about twice as wide as high. Beaded spiral cords. Low or slightly raised spire. Thick, oval, calcareous operculum.
Color: Cream to tan exterior. Iridescent silver interior.
Habitat: Offshore on rocky or shelly bottoms. Collected by scuba divers at depths greater than 60 feet.
Range: Cape Lookout, N.C., to Florida and Brazil.
Notes: Also called a **longspine star shell**. Females release eggs into the water. Young are free-swimming.

TOP-SHAPED – topsnails (Trochidae)

beautiful topsnail

• **beautiful topsnail** *Calliostoma pulchrum* (C.B. Adams)
Description: (1/2 inch wide) Tiny shell shaped like a top or cone with flat sides. Length and width of shell nearly equal. Surface not rough but has beaded spiral ridges stronger near the whorl sutures. No umbilicus. Round or elliptical aperture. Operculum.
Color: Yellow-brown exterior with reddish spots. Iridescent interior.
Habitat: Lives in sounds and just offshore. Occasionally found on sound and ocean beaches.
Range: North Carolina to Florida.
Notes: Also called a **beautiful top shell**. This species is a herbivore. Young are free-swimming. Topsnails are difficult to identify. Most are found in areas not readily accessible to the average collector.

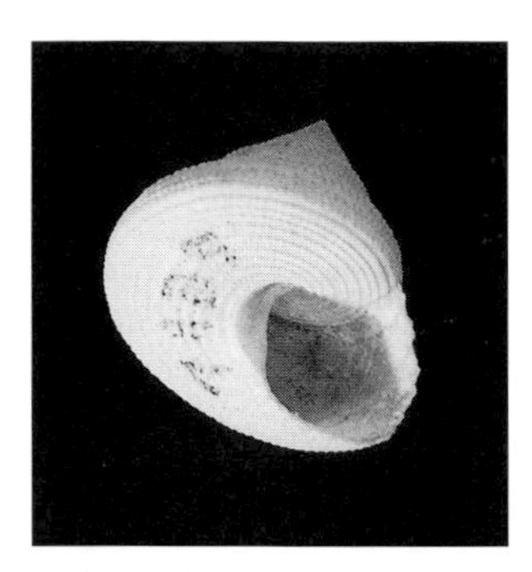

sculptured topsnail

• **sculptured topsnail** *Calliostoma euglyptum* (A. Adams)
Description: (1 inch wide) Similar in shape to the **beautiful topsnail** but larger with beaded spiral ridges of equal strength (not stronger near whorl sutures). Rounded body whorl. Round or elliptical aperture. Operculum. No umbilicus.
Color: Yellow-brown or pinkish exterior, sometimes with dark brown bars running the width of the whorl. Iridescent interior.
Habitat: Lives near inlet rock jetties and offshore. Rarely found on ocean beaches.
Range: North Carolina to Texas.
Notes: See **beautiful topsnail** ***Notes***.

depressed topsnail

• **depressed topsnail** *Calliostoma yucatecanum* Dall
Description: (1/2 inch wide) Small shell shaped like a top or cone with flat sides. Many spiral cords. Rounded body whorl. Broader than the **sculptured topsnail** with a deep umbilicus. Round or elliptical aperture. Operculum.
Color: Yellow to pink exterior with dark spots or bars. Iridescent interior.
Habitat: Lives offshore.
Range: North Carolina to Yucatan.
Notes: Also called a **Yucatan top shell**. See **beautiful topsnail** ***Notes***.

TOP-SHAPED – sundials (Architectonicidae)

common sundial

• **common sundial** *Architectonica nobilis* Röding (= *A. granulata* Lamarck)
Description: (2 1/4 inches wide) Round, broad shell; top-shaped and somewhat flattened (as if only the top portion of a shell present). Prominent beaded spiral cords on top and bottom. Rounded or elliptical aperture. Deep, crenulated, funnel-shaped hole (umbilicus) under shell. Horny operculum.
Color: Whitish exterior with spiral rows of brown spots. Brown operculum.
Habitat: Lives offshore south of Cape Hatteras (particularly between Cape Hatteras and Cape Lookout). Rarely found on ocean beaches.
Range: North Carolina to Brazil.
Notes: This species' feeding habits are uncertain. Its long free-swimming stage results in wide dispersal.

UNUSUAL GASTROPODS – slippersnails (Crepidulidae)

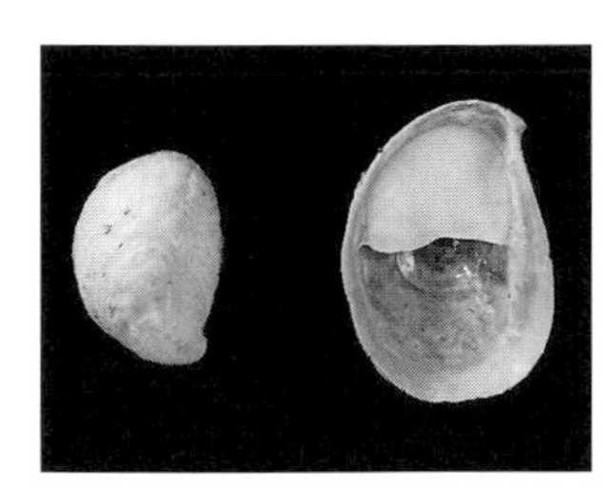

common Atlantic slippersnail

• **common Atlantic slippersnail** *Crepidula fornicata* (Linnaeus)

Description: (2 1/2 inches) Slightly arched cap-shaped shell with an oval base. Appearance of a slipper or small boat with a small shelf or deck underneath. Pointed end of the deck not deep in the shell. Smooth or slightly wrinkled exterior. When living, often attached to others.

Color: Buff exterior with small brownish specks. Buff interior sometimes lightly flecked with brown. White shelf.

Habitat: Lives offshore. Common on sound and ocean beaches.

Range: Nova Scotia, Canada, to Texas.

Notes: Also called a **boat shell** or **quarterdeck**. Its shape varies, depending on the shape of the shell to which it attaches. This species is a filter feeder. It may take over oyster beds and smother the mollusks. A hermaphrodite, it alternates sex during spawning season. Often, it lives in piles, on top of others, with large females at the bottom and males at the top. Below Cape Hatteras, it is uncommon to see strings of three or more slippersnails on top of one other. Females produce capsulelike eggs, attach them to a rock and brood them until they hatch. Larvae are free-swimming.

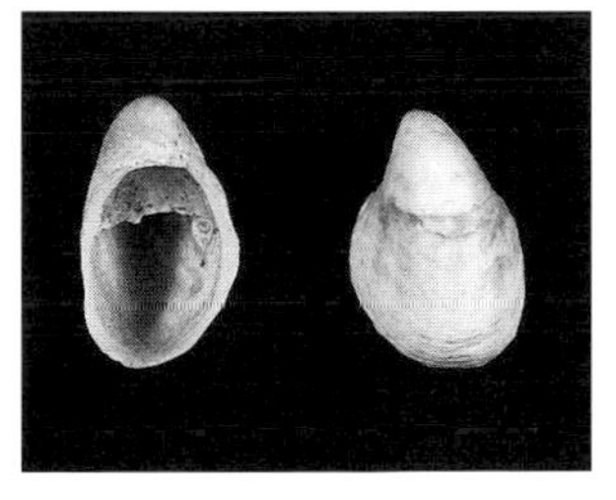

convex slippersnail

• **convex slippersnail** *Crepidula convexa* Say

Description: (1/2 inch) Cap-shaped shell with a strong arch and an oval base. A prominent apex curves around like an elf's cap. A shelf or deck underneath is set deep in the shell. Wrinkled exterior. Not found attached to others.

Color: Brownish exterior with specks of reddish brown. Reddish brown interior.

Habitat: Lives offshore. Occasionally found on offshore beaches.

Range: Massachusetts to Texas.

Notes: This species is a filter feeder. A hermaphrodite, it alternates sex during spawning season. Sex is influenced by hormones released by the opposite sex. Females produce capsulelike eggs, attach them to a rock and brood them until they hatch. Larvae are free-swimming.

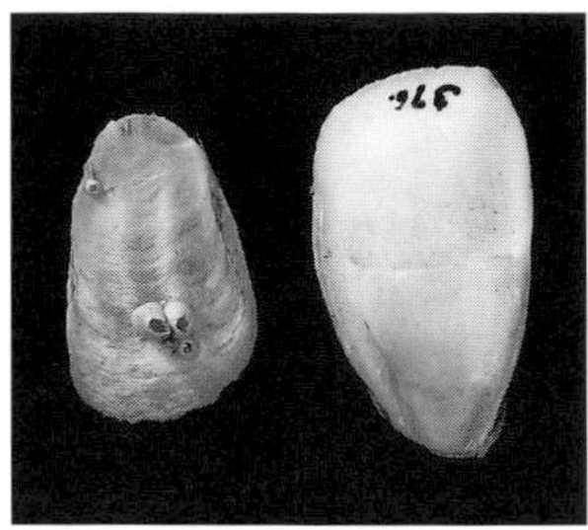
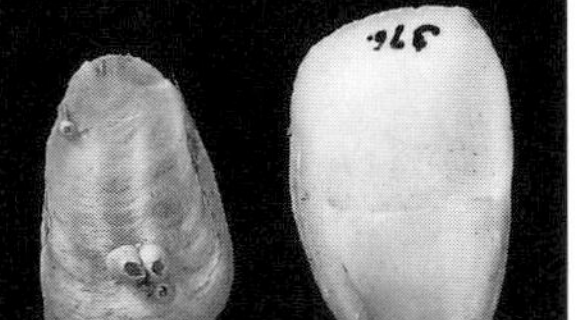

eastern white slippersnail

• **eastern white slippersnail** *Crepidula plana* (Say) (= *C. unguiformis* Lamarck)
Description: (1 1/2 inches) Cap-shaped, flat or concave shell (shape acquired from frequently living inside empty snail shells). Oval to elongate base with a small, convex shelf or deck underneath. Wrinkled exterior with concentric lines.
Color: White exterior and interior. Glossy interior.
Habitat: Lives in sounds and offshore. Commonly found washed onto sound and ocean beaches.
Range: Nova Scotia, Canada, to Brazil.
Notes: Also called a **flat slipper shell**. This species attaches to the inside of dead shells, especially *Busycon* and *Polinices* species (even if a hermit crab is using the dead shell as a home). Also see **convex slippersnail** ***Notes***.

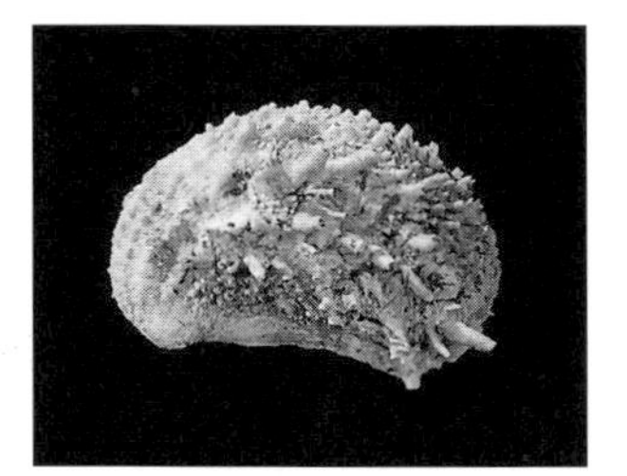

spiny slippersnail

• **spiny slippersnail** *Crepidula aculeata* (Gmelin)
Description: (1 inch) Cap-shaped shell with a small shelf or deck underneath. Attaches to rock or shell. North Carolina's only slippersnail with a rough or spiny exterior.
Color: Exterior orange to brown, mottled or rayed with white. Polished, whitish interior mottled or rayed with brown. Whitish shelf or deck.
Habitat: Occasionally washed onto ocean beaches south of Cape Hatteras.
Range: North Carolina to Brazil.
Notes: Also called a **thorny slipper shell**. See **convex slippersnail** ***Notes***.

spotted slippersnail

• **spotted slippersnail** *Crepidula maculosa* Conrad
Description: (1 inch) Similar to the **common Atlantic slippersnail** except more heavily spotted. Fairly straight edge on shelf.
Color: Exterior and interior white to buff with many small, reddish brown spots. White shelf.
Habitat: Lives offshore near the Gulf Stream on dead penshells. Might be found on ocean beaches.
Range: North Carolina to the Gulf of Mexico.
Notes: See **convex slippersnail** ***Notes***.

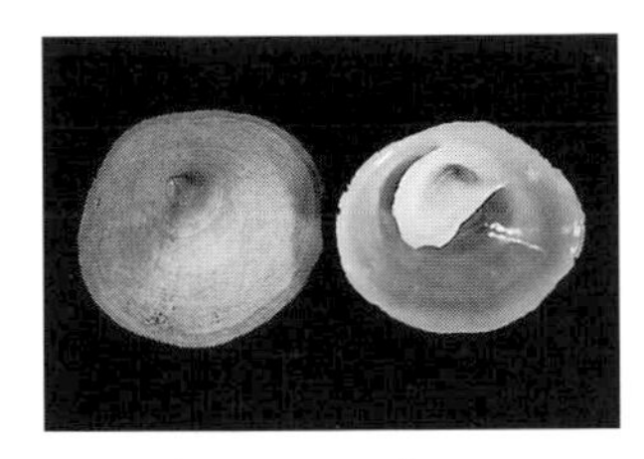

striate cup-and-saucer

• **striate cup-and-saucer** *Crucibulum striatum* Say
Description: (1 1/2 inches wide) Cap-shaped shell with round base and a small oval cap under one side of the shell. Many wavy, radial ridges on exterior. Apex near center and slightly twisted.
Color: Exterior pinkish gray to yellowish brown. Interior yellow to orange-brown. Shelf or deck white.
Habitat: Lives offshore attached to **sea scallops**. Occasionally found on ocean beaches.
Range: Canada to Brazil.
Notes: Also called a **cup and saucer limpet**. See **convex slippersnail** ***Notes***. Specimens from North Carolina waters have been found north of Cape Lookout.

UNUSUAL GASTROPODS – carriersnails (Xenophoridae)

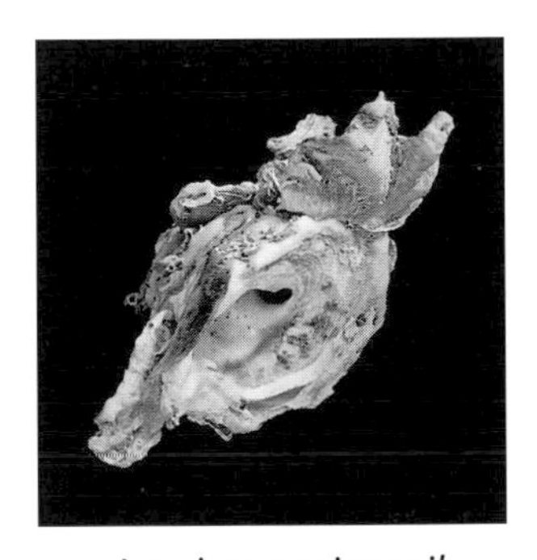

American carriersnail

• **American carriersnail** *Xenophora conchyliophora* (Born)
Description: (2 1/4 inches wide) Top-shaped, broadly conical shell. Shape rarely seen because covered with attached pieces of shell, stone or coral, giving it the appearance of a small pile of shells or debris. Rounded or elliptical aperture.
Color: Yellowish exterior with brown swirls. Brownish interior.
Habitat: Lives offshore. Has been found in **Atlantic calico scallop** beds.
Range: North Carolina to Brazil.
Notes: Also called a **common carrier shell**. This species feeds on detritus and algae. The family name means "carrier of strangers." Often called the "original shell collector," it attaches shells using a special cement that is sticky underwater. As it grows, it continues to add shells around its bottom. Although it is usually assumed that the shell and debris are added for camouflage, some investigators think the projections may also help the animal move over the ocean floor.

Squids, Tuskshells & Chitons

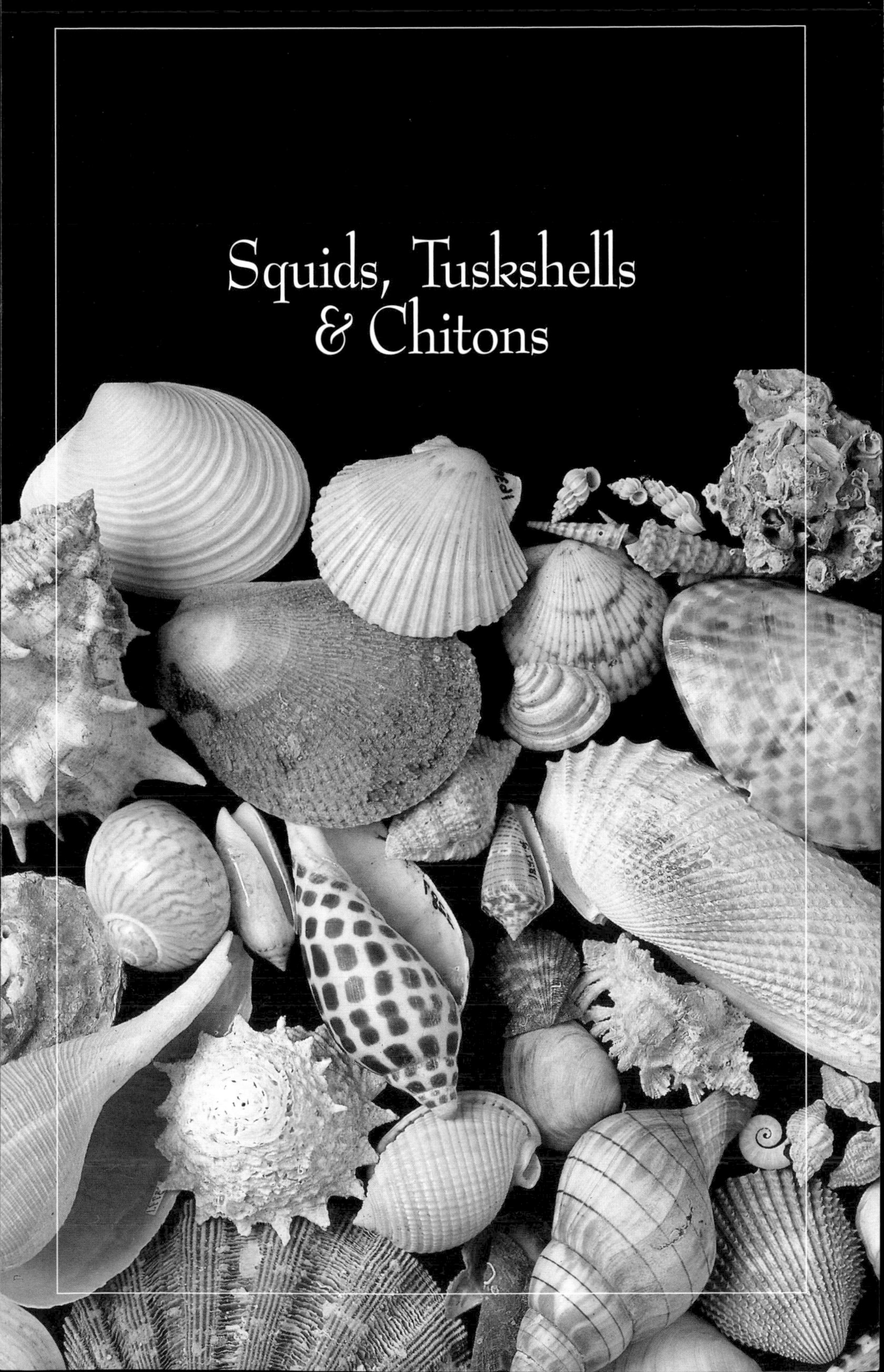

SQUIDS – ram's horns (Spirulidae)

ram's horn squid

• **ram's horn squid** *Spirula spirula* (Linnaeus)
Description: (1 inch) Flat, fragile, loosely coiled shell resembling a ram's horn. Interior partitioned into chambers.
Color: Pure white exterior and interior.
Habitat: Lives offshore. Occasionally washed onto ocean beaches.
Range: Worldwide.
Notes: Also called a **common spirula**. This shell forms inside a living deep-sea squid. Its inner chambers are filled with gas, causing the shell to float when the animal dies.

TUSKSHELLS – (Dentaliidae)

ivory tuskshell

• **ivory tuskshell** *Graptacme eborea* (Conrad)
(= *Dentalium eboreum*)
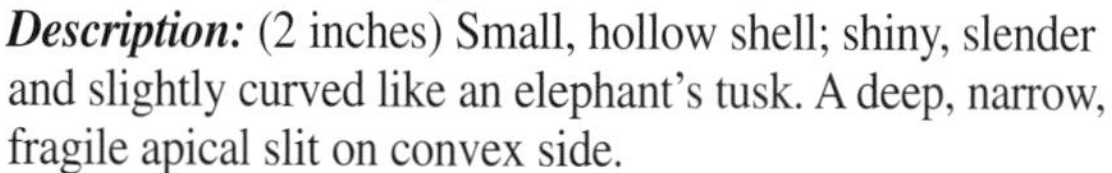
Description: (2 inches) Small, hollow shell; shiny, slender and slightly curved like an elephant's tusk. A deep, narrow, fragile apical slit on convex side.
Color: Glossy white to pinkish.
Habitat: Lives buried in mud or sand in deep water. Occasionally washed onto ocean beaches, most often in the high or low tide drift lines.
Range: North Carolina to Brazil.
Notes: Only the narrow end of the shell protrudes from the mud. A carnivore, it uses its lobed appendages to capture tiny bivalves and other organisms. Eggs and sperm are released into the water, and fertilization takes place there. Young are free-swimming. Water enters and waste leaves through a hole in the aboveground part of the shell. Twenty-four kinds of tuskshells have been recorded off the North Carolina coast; most of them are small, difficult to identify and from deep water.

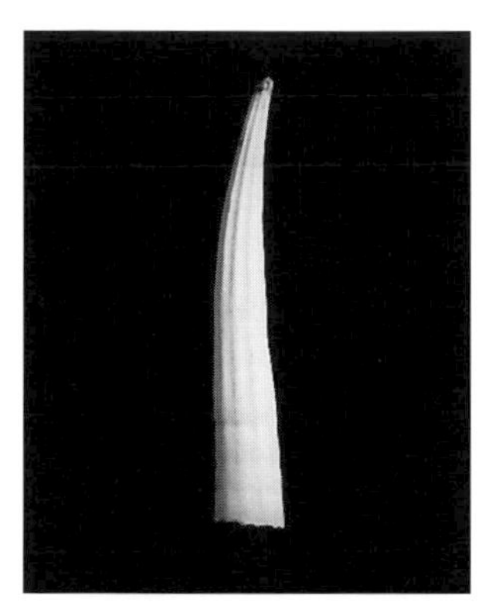

reticulate tuskshell

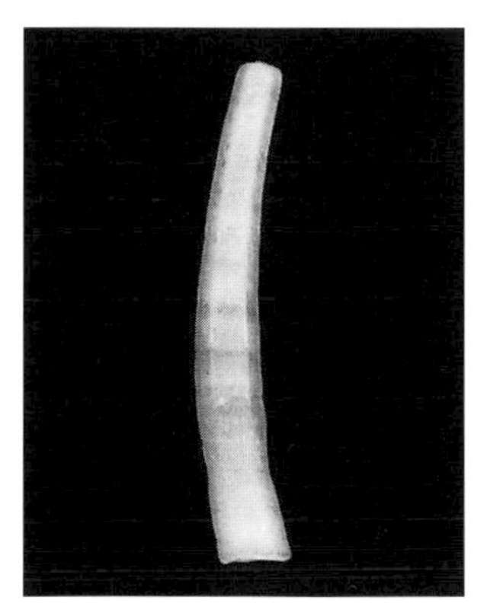

American tuskshell

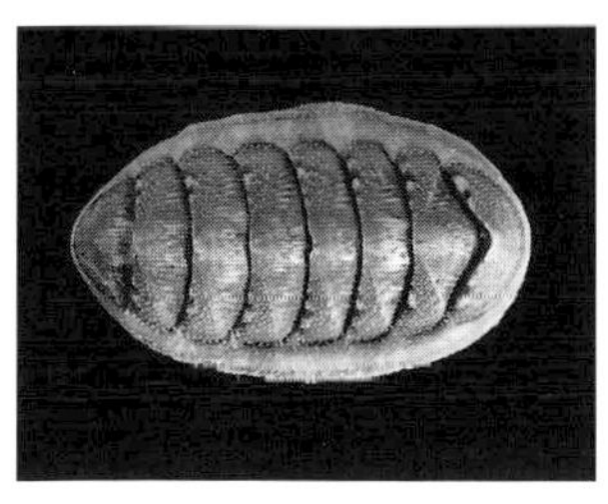

eastern beaded chiton

• **reticulate tuskshell** *Dentalium laqueatum* A.E. Verrill
Description: (2 inches) Small, hollow, tusklike shell with nine to 12 strong ribs running the length of the shell but fading toward one end. Concave spaces between ribs. Curved apex.
Color: Dull white.
Habitat: Lives in deep offshore waters (200 to 750 feet deep).
Range: North Carolina to Brazil.
Notes: This is North Carolina's largest and heaviest tuskshell. Also see **ivory tuskshell *Notes***.

• **American tuskshell** *Dentalium americanum* Chenu (= *D. texasianum* Philippi)
Description: (1 inch) Hollow, tusklike shell. Slender and curved. Hexagonal in cross section. Six ribs running the length of the shell. Flat, broad spaces between ribs.
Color: Dull grayish white.
Habitat: Lives buried in mud or sand in deep water. Occasionally washed up in the high or low tide drift lines of sound or ocean beaches.
Range: North Carolina to Brazil.
Notes: Also called a **Texas tusk**. See **ivory tuskshell *Notes***.

CHITONS – eastern beaded chitons (Chaetopleuridae)

• **eastern beaded chiton** *Chaetopleura apiculata* (Say)
Description: (1 inch) Flattened oval mollusk covered by eight shelly valves or plates encircled by a girdle. Valves angled toward the center and have up to 20 longitudinal rows of raised beads. Girdle beaded with scattered, short, microscopic hairs.
Color: Light gray, sometimes reddish.
Habitat: Lives attached to shells in shelly areas of high-salinity lagoons, sounds, estuarine mouths and intertidal beaches of offshore islands. Rarely seen on ocean beaches.
Range: Massachusetts to Florida.
Notes: Also called the **common eastern chiton**. A flattened foot attaches the chiton to hard substrates.

CHITONS –
striolate chitons (Ischnochitonidae)

striolate chiton
(on shell surface
near the beak)

* • **striolate chiton** *Ischnochiton striolatus* (J.E. Gray) (= *I. papillosus* C.B. Adams, *I. squamulosa* C.B. Adams)
Description: (1/2 inch) Similar to **eastern beaded chiton** except smaller. Differs from young **eastern beaded chiton** in having randomly placed beads on its outer surface — not longitudinal rows of raised beads. Also in this species, the girdle is covered with overlaying scales — the surface is not grainy with short hairs as in the **eastern beaded chiton**.
Color: Whitish, mottled with greenish brown.
Habitat: Lives in mouth of inlets on shelly bottoms. Known in intertidal area of Beaufort Inlet and in Cape Lookout Bight.
Range: North Carolina, lower Florida and West Indies.
Notes: Also called a **mesh-pitted chiton**.

Color
Photographs

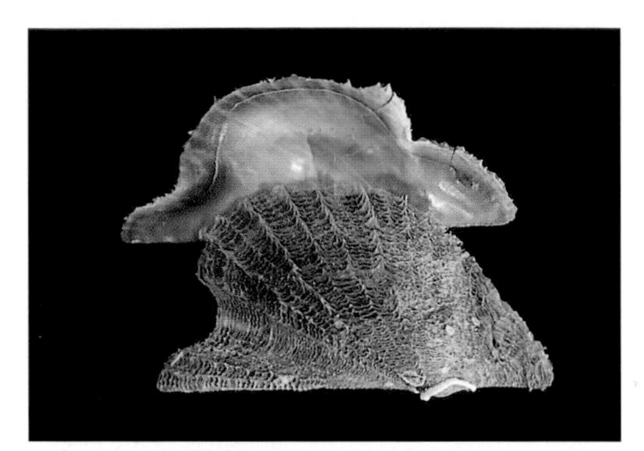

Atlantic wing-oyster
Pteria colymbus

lions-paw scallop
Nodipecten nodosus

rough scallop
Aequipecten muscosus

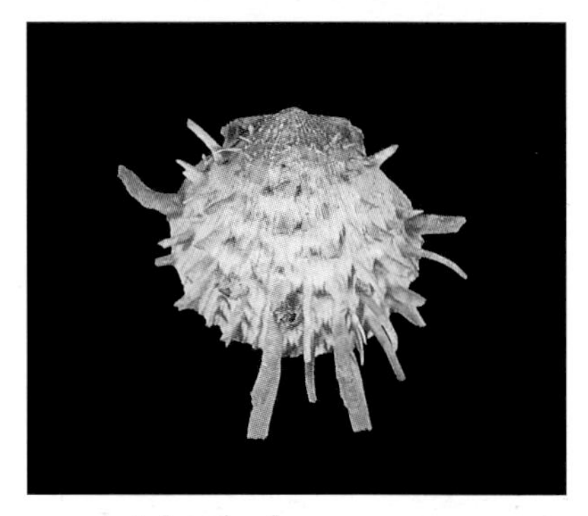

Atlantic thorny-oyster
Spondylus americanus

shiny dwarf-tellin
Tellina nitens

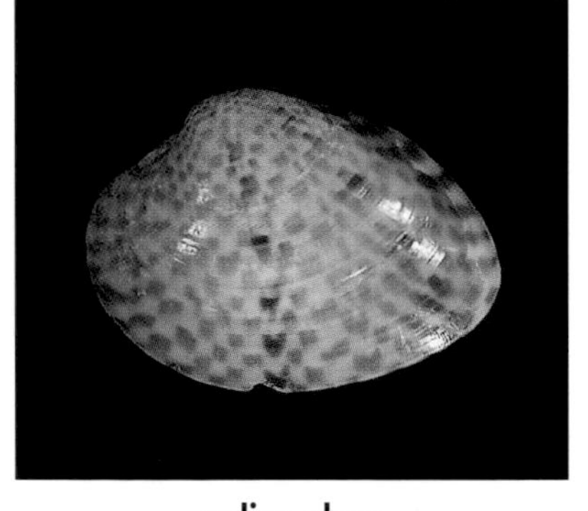

calico clam
Macrocallista maculata

Atlantic awningclam
Solemya velum

Florida fighting conch
Strombus alatus

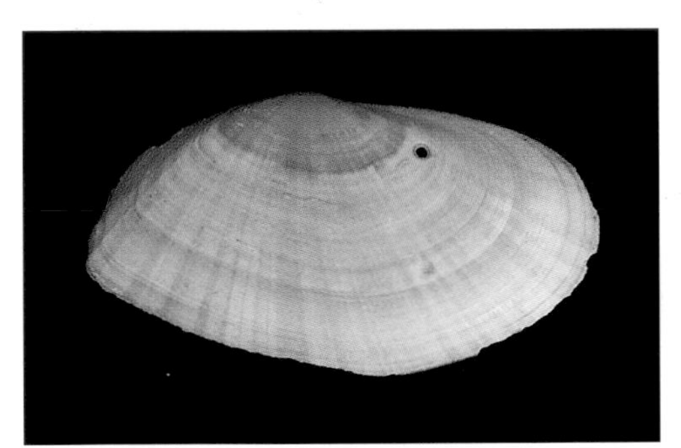

great-tellin
Tellina magna

milk conch
Strombus costatus

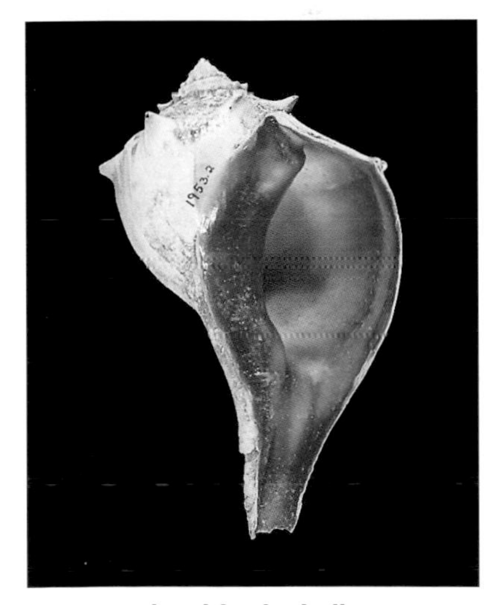

knobbed whelk
Busycon carica

Atlantic trumpet triton
Charonia tritonis variegata

eastern auger
Terebra dislocata

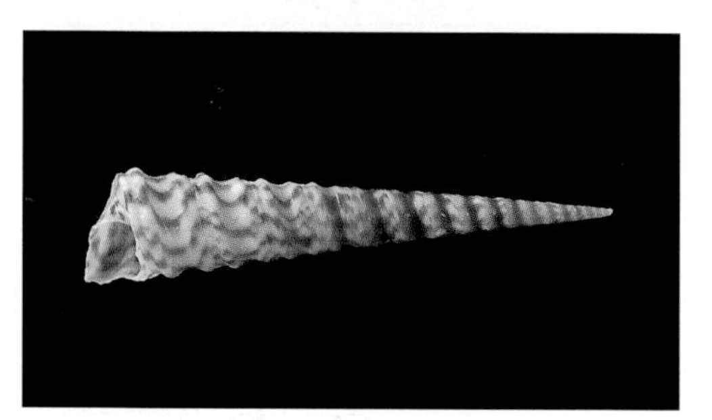

eastern turretsnail
Turritella exoleta

true tulip
Fasciolaria tulipa

banded tulip
Fasciolaria lilium hunteria

Kreb triton
Cymatium corrugatum krebsii

Simpson drillia
Cerodrillia simpsoni

Sozon cone
Conus delessertii

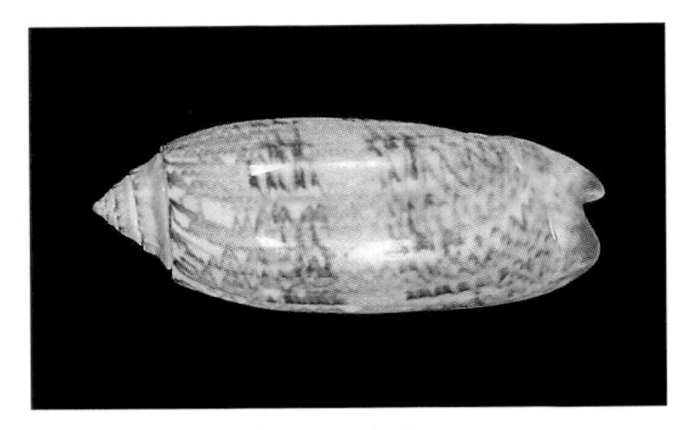

lettered olive
Oliva sayana

ribbed cantharus
Cantharus multangulus

harlequin miter
Vexillum histrio

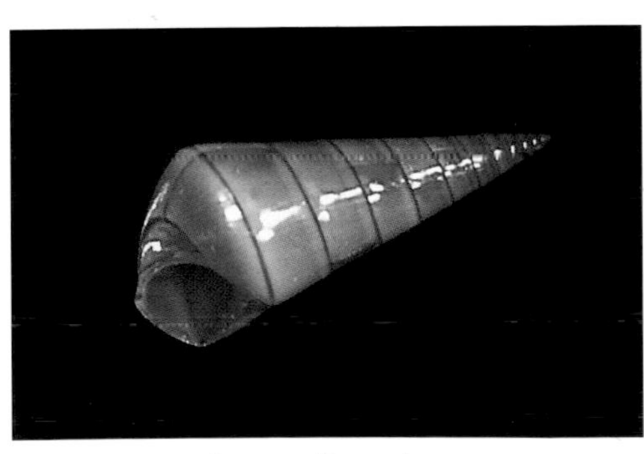

brown-line niso
Niso aeglees

Floridensis cone
Conus floridensis floridensis

junonia
Scaphella junonia

seaboard marginella
Marginella roscida

reticulate cowrie-helmet
Cypraecassis testiculus

Atlantic deer cowrie
Cypraea cervus

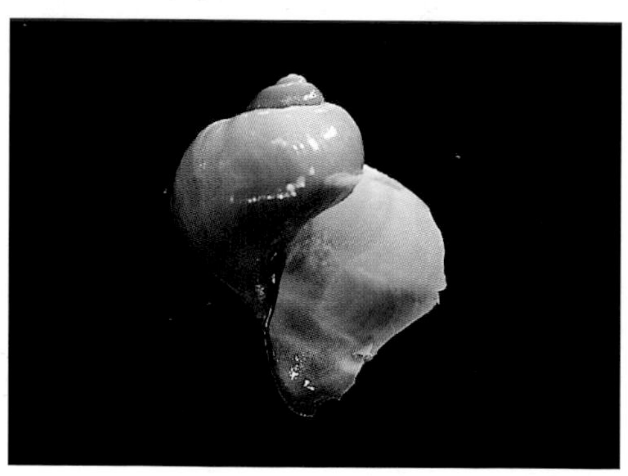

elongate janthina
Janthina globosa

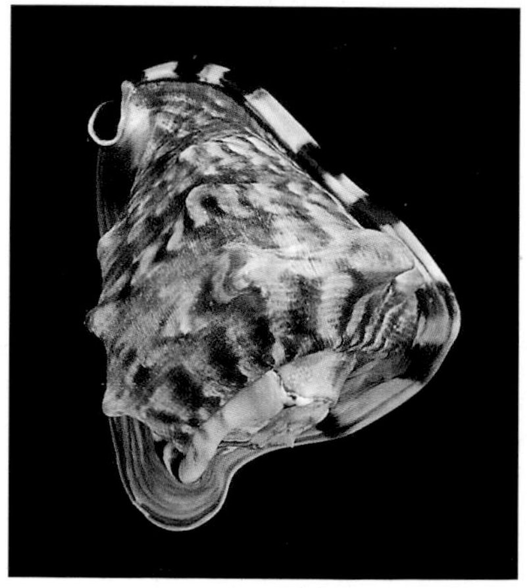

Caribbean helmet
Cassis tuberosa

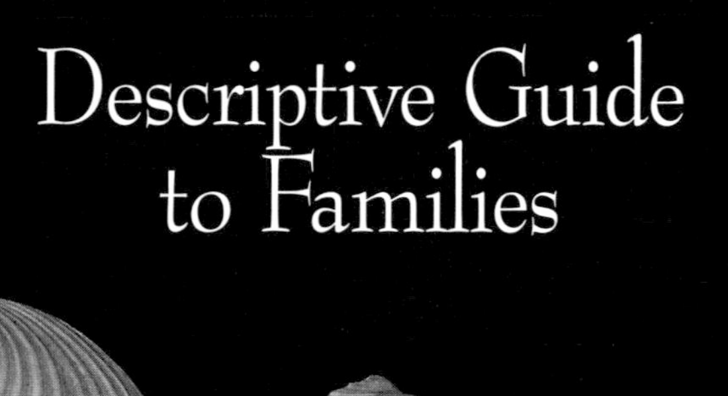
Descriptive Guide
to Families

Order of families is by shape and not taxonomic relationship. The descriptions are very general due to the wide character variability within most molluscan families.

Bivalves

• **ark-shaped:** "piano" hinge (series of teeth positioned next to one another like keys on a piano), taxodont dentation ***Pages 12 to 16***

Arcidae	(arks)	straight piano hinge; thick shell
Glycymerididae	(bittersweets)	curved piano hinge; thick shell
Nuculidae	(nutclams)	pearly inside; small; rounded
Nuculanidae	(nutclams, yoldias)	thin; not pearly inside; small; elongated

• **cockle-shaped:** round, oval; beak pointing upward; no pallial sinus ***Pages 17 to 20***

Cardiidae	(cockles)	narrow radial ribs or smooth eggshell-like surface
Carditidae	(carditas)	broad radial ribs

• **oyster-shaped:** irregular, lumpy shape ***Pages 20 to 25***

Pteriidae	(wing-oysters, pearl-oysters)	winglike extension of long hinge line
Ostreidae	(oysters)	porcelainlike shell
Plicatulidae	(kittenpaws)	resembles a cat's outstretched paw
Chamidae	(jewelboxes)	thick shell; leafy or spiny ridges; one or both valves deeply cupped
Anomiidae	(jingles)	translucent; hole in one valve

• **scallop-shaped:** hinge has two "ears" ***Pages 25 to 28***

Spondylidae	(thorny-oysters)	long spines; small ears
Pectinidae	(scallops)	broad, rounded shell; large ears
Limidae	(fileclams)	broad, oval shell; small ears

• **mussel-shaped:** narrow, fan shape; beak near narrow end ***Pages 28 to 32***

Mytilidae	(mussels)	inside pearly
Gastrochaenidae	(gastrochaenas, rocellarias)	wide gape along most of lower edge

• **penshell-shaped:** large, thin, brittle, fan-shaped; radial ribs, some with spines ***Page 33***

Pinnidae	(penshells)

- **clam-shaped:** round, oval, triangular or slightly elongate shells *Pages 34 to 54*

Veneridae	(venus clams, quahogs, dosinias, cyclinellas)	egg- or heart-shaped; beak points toward front; prominent cardinal and lateral teeth; pallial sinus
Arcticidae	(ocean quahogs)	like venus clams but missing lunule and pallial sinus
Mactridae	(surfclams)	oval-shaped shell; hinge has spoon-shaped depression
Corbiculidae	(marshclams)	surface usually has eroded areas
Corbulidae	(corbulas)	small, thick shell; one valve overlaps the other
Myidae	(soft-shell clams)	thin shell; horizontally projecting shelf on one valve
Crassatellidae	(crassinellas)	thick shell; two cardinal teeth; concentric ridges on surface
Semelidae	(semeles, abras)	small spoon-shaped cavity in hinge; round pallial sinus
Lucinidae	(lucines)	long, narrow muscle scar; no pallial sinus
Ungulinidae	(diplodons)	two cardinal teeth (one is split); small and round
Tellinidae	(tellins, macomas, strigillas)	thin-shelled, one end might be slightly twisted; two cardinal teeth, sometimes without lateral teeth
Donacidae	(coquinas)	colorful; wedge-shaped; lives in tidal zone of beaches
Mesodesmatidae	(wedgeclams, ervilias)	small, oval; many concentric ridges
Periplomatidae	(spoonclams)	thin shell; pearly; spoonlike groove; pallial sinus; no hinge teeth
Pandoridae	(pandoras)	flat, pearly shell; no pallial sinus; strong cardinal teeth
Lyonsiidae	(lyonsias)	thin shell; pearly; no hinge teeth; misshapen
Hiatellidae	(geoducks)	large, thick shell with squared-off end

- **angelwing-shaped:** resembles an angel's wing *Pages 54 to 56*

Pholadidae	(angelwings, mud-piddocks, piddocks)	front of top edge is rolled out; no hinge teeth
Petricolidae	(rupellarias, false angelwing)	cardinal hinge teeth

- **razor-shaped:** rectangular *Pages 56 to 58*

Solecurtidae	(tagelus, corrugate solecurtus)	top and bottom edges parallel; beak almost central
Solenidae	(jackknives)	long and narrow; beak at anterior end
Solemyidae	(awningclams)	fragile shell; tough, fringed or rayed periostracum

Gastropods

• **whelk-shaped:** large body whorl; elongate aperture that narrows to a long canal
Pages 60 to 70

Melongenidae	(whelks, conchs)	most with shouldered whorls
Ficidae	(figsnails)	almost no spire; crisscross sculpture
Strombidae	(true conchs)	heavy, flared outer lip with notch at bottom
Fasciolariidae	(tulips, conchs)	graceful, spindle-shaped shell; elongate spire
Ranellidae	(tritons, distortios)	aperture has teeth
Muricidae	(murexes, drills, rocksnails)	thick shell; axial ribs may develop long spines; inner aperture wall smooth

• **auger-shaped:** high spire; small aperture ***Pages 70 to 80***

Terebridae	(augers)	sharply pointed spire; notchlike aperture
Turritellidae	(turretsnails, wormsnails)	sharply pointed spire; round aperture; later whorls may be loose
Epitoniidae	(wentletraps)	round aperture; whorls sculptured
Cerithiidae	(ceriths and bittums)	bluntly pointed spires
Cerithiopsidae	(miniature ceriths)	small, sharply pointed spire; concave base
Pyramidellidae	(pyrams, odostomes)	small oval aperture
Turridae	(turrids, drillias, mangelias, oxias)	small notch at top of outer aperture lip
Eulimidae	(eulimas)	acutely conical, glossy surface

• **mudsnail-shaped:** short, spindle-shaped shells; small apertures ***Pages 80 to 87***

Nassariidae	(mudsnails, nassas, dog whelks, basket shells)	beaded or rough surface
Columbellidae	(dovesnails)	spindle-shaped with spire longer than aperture
Cancellariidae	(nutmegs)	beaded or ribbed; whorls have distinct shoulders
Bursidae	(frogsnails)	thick outer lip with teeth; one side appears flattened
Littorinidae	(periwinkles)	rounded aperture
Buccinidae	(colus, cantharus)	well-developed spire; smooth inner aperture lip
Coralliophilidae	(coralsnails)	scaly spiral cords
Costellariidae	(miters)	sharply pointed spire; folds on inner aperture lip

• **olive-shaped:** cylindrical or cone-shaped; narrow aperture extends length (or almost length) of shell *Pages 88 to 96*

Olividae	(olives)	cylindrical with narrow aperture
Conidae	(cones)	cone-shaped, moderate spire
Marginellidae	(marginellas)	pear-shaped, tiny spire
Volutidae	(volutes, junonia)	elongate, spotted shell
Melampodidae	(melampi)	small, fat shell; cone-shaped spire; salt marsh habitat
Cypraeidae	(cowries)	aperture lips lined with small, evenly spaced teeth
Triviidae	(trivias)	surface resembles corduroy (rows of ridges around shell)
Ovulidae	(simnias, cyphomas)	resembles a mouth with smooth lips
Bullidae	(bubbles)	globular lower end of aperture is wider than upper end
Scaphandridae	(barrel-bubbles)	olive-shaped; aperture widens at the end

• **helmet-shaped:** large body whorl *Pages 96 to 98*

Cassidae	(helmets, Scotch bonnet)	parietal shield; both aperture lips with teeth
Tonnidae	(tuns)	light but strong shell; no parietal shield

• **moonsnail-shaped:** globe-shaped shell; low spire *Pages 99 to 102*

Naticidae	(moonsnails, shark eye, baby-ears)	umbilicus and callus
Janthinidae	(janthinas)	purple; fragile; outer lip curved

• **top-shaped:** shell width can be greater than shell height *Pages 102 to 104*

Fissurellidae	(keyhole limpets)	resembles a coolie hat
Turbinidae	(turbans, starsnails)	resembles a turban; interior iridescent
Trochidae	(topsnails)	resembles a toy top; beaded spiral cords; interior not iridescent
Architectonicidae	(sundials)	appears to be only the top of a shell; large crenulated umbilicus

• **unusual gastropods:** *Pages 105 to 107*

Crepidulidae	(slippersnails, striate cup-and-saucer)	resembles a boat or slipper; shelly platform inserted into aperture
Xenophoridae	(carriersnails)	appears to be a pile of shell debris; aperture underneath

• squids: *Page 110*

Spirulidae	(ram's horns)	fragile; coiled shell with chambers

• tuskshells: tusk-shaped *Pages 110 to 111*

Dentaliidae	(tuskshells)	

• chitons: elongate oval; eight overlapping shell plates; leathery or scaly girdle *Pages 111 to 112*

Chaetopleuridae	(eastern beaded chiton)	beaded girdle
Ischnochitonidae	(striolate chiton)	small girdle covered by scales

Glossary

• **accessory plates** — small, shelly plates over the hinge of some bivalves

• **algae** — group of simple, nonvascular, photosynthetic aquatic plants having single-celled sex organs

• **aperture** — opening in a gastropod shell or tuskshell through which the animal can protrude

• **apex** — pointed tip of a gastropod shell that indicates where the shell began growing

• **axial ribs** — ribs that run lengthwise (not spiral) on a gastropod shell

• **beak** — pointed part of a bivalve shell near the hinge where the shell began growing

• **bivalve** — mollusk with two shells joined by a hinge (such as a clam or oyster); no head or radula

• **body whorl** — last and usually largest whorl of a gastropod shell

• **byssus** — thread produced by some bivalve mollusks to attach themselves to rocks or other stable objects

• **callus** — a thickened calcareous surface, frequently on inner aperture

• **cardinal teeth** — vertical teeth on a bivalve hinge just below the beak

• **carina** — keel-like structure

• **carnivore** — animal that feeds on other animals

• **chevron-shaped** — a V-shaped or inverted V-shaped pattern

• **chiton** — mollusk covered by a linear series of eight shell plates; a head and radula are present

• **concentric** — ribs or lines that curve parallel to the bottom edge of some bivalve shells, forming semicircles around the beak area

• **conchiolin** — a protein substance that is a basic ingredient in the formation of a shell

• **coral** — animal that lives in colonies and secretes a hard outer calcareous skeleton; large numbers of them may form a coral reef

• **crenulations** — grooved or scalloped areas along the bottom edge of a shell

• **deposit feeders** — animals that feed on organic matter in particle-filled sediments

• **detritivores** — animals that feed on detritus

• **detritus** — tiny particles of matter, usually bits of dead plants or animals in sediments or suspended in water

• **ears** — earlike extension of bivalve hinge

• **echinoderm** — group of marine animals with stiff, spiny body walls (includes sea urchins, sand dollars and sea stars (starfish))

• **estuary** — brackish area where salt water from the ocean meets freshwater drainage from the land

• **flammule** — small flamelike streak of color

• **gastropod** — single shell (univalve) mollusk with a head and radula — usually with a spiral growth pattern (such as a conch or whelk); some sluglike mollusks (sea hares, nudibranchs) have a shell only as a larva

• **girdle** — in chitons, the muscular, leathery band that surrounds eight shelly plates

• **growth lines** — lines or thickened areas of the shell that form at the end of a growth period

• **herbivore** — animal that feeds on plants (a vegetarian)

• **hermaphrodite** — animal that has both male and female sex organs

• **hinge** — area where the two valves of a bivalve are joined by a ligament

• **inflated** — puffed up or swollen-looking

• **intertidal** — area between the high tide and the low tide lines

• **iridescent** — pearly, shiny surface that displays a rainbow of colors in the light

• **jetties** — structures built to alter currents or protect an area from waves

• **larva** (plural: larvae) — growth stage that many types of mollusks enter after hatching from eggs

• **lateral teeth** — horizontal teeth on the sides of a bivalve's hinge

• **ligament** — elastic hinge cartilage that holds together the two valves of a bivalve

• **lip** — inside or outside edge of the aperture in a gastropod shell

• **lunule** — heart-shaped depression in front of the beaks of some bivalves; one half of the heart on each valve

• **mantle** — fleshy tissue covering the soft parts of the mollusk; secretes the material that creates the shell and its colors; also involved in respiration

• **muscle scar** — slight depression inside a bivalve shell where a muscle was attached

• **nacreous** — made of nacre, or mother-of-pearl, which is iridescent or pearly

• **nuclear whorl** — the first few tiny whorls of a gastropod shell that were present when the mollusk hatched

• **omnivore** — animal that feeds on both plants and animals

• **operculum** — "trap door" in some types of gastropods; used to close the aperture and protect the gastropod when it is frightened or out of the water

• **pallial line** — line that runs parallel to the bottom edge of some bivalve shells, indicating where the mantle's edge was attached to the shell

• **pallial sinus** — indentation in the pallial line that indicates where the edge of the mantle was pushed in to make room for the siphons (small pallial sinuses indicate short siphons and shallow-burrowing bivalves; large pallial sinuses indicate long siphons and deep-burrowing bivalves)

• **parietal shield** — thickened portion of the inner aperture lip of a gastropod

• **periostracum** — outer "skin" covering a live shell

• **proboscis** — a tubelike extension on a gastropod's head that has a mouth and a ribbonlike strip of teeth (radula) for feeding

• **radial** — ribs or lines that start at the beak and radiate toward the edge of some bivalve shells

• **radula** — ribbonlike structure of teeth in the proboscis of gastropods, used for scraping or tearing food or drilling holes through the shell of prey

• **salinity** — degree of saltiness of water

• **scavenger** — animal that feeds on dead and decaying plants and animals

• **shoulder** — angular upper part of a whorl, most frequently just below a suture

• **siphon** — retractable, tubelike extension of the mantle through which water enters and leaves, bringing in food and oxygen and expelling wastes

• **spiral ribs** — ribs arranged in a spiral pattern around gastropod shells

• **spire** — all the whorls above the body whorl in a gastropod

• **strombid notch** — shallow notch on lower lip of aperture, provides right eye of conch a protected view port

• **suspension feeders** — bivalves that feed using their siphons to draw in food particles suspended in the water

• **suture** — on a gastropod, the juncture around the spire where one whorl meets the next (usually above the whorl shoulder)

• **taxodont** — linear series of many small transverse teeth on hinge

• **truncate** — an end of a shell that is squarely cut off

• **turrid notch** — characteristic notch on the upper portion of the outer lip of gastropods in the family Turridae

• **umbilicus** — funnel-like opening on the base of some gastropods

• **valve** — one of the two shells of a bivalve

• **wampum** — shells or parts of shells placed on a string and used for money by early Native Americans

• **whorl** — one full turn of a gastropod shell

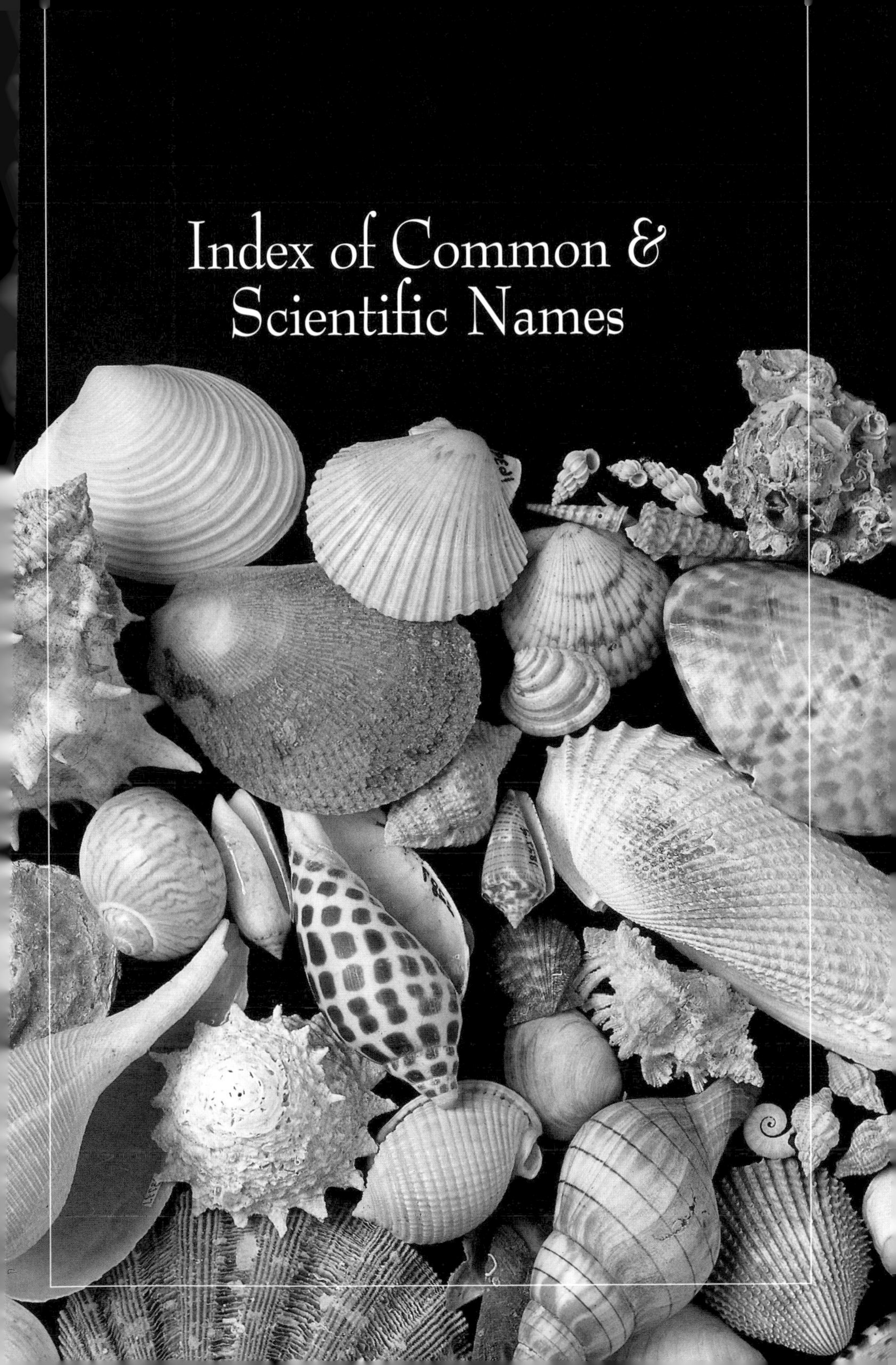

Index of Common & Scientific Names

Bibliography

• Abbott, R. Tucker. 1974. *American Seashells*. Second edition. Van Nostrand Reinhold Co. Inc., New York, N.Y. 541 pp.

• Abbott, R. Tucker. 1986. *Seashells of North America: A Guide to Field Identification.* Western Publ. Co. Inc., Racine, Wis. 280 pp.

• Andrews, J. 1971. *Seashells of the Texas Coast.* Univ. Texas Press, Austin, Texas. 298 pp.

• Carson, Rachel. 1955. *The Edge of the Sea.* Houghton Mifflin Co., Boston, Mass. 276 pp.

• Carson, Rachel. 1951. *The Sea Around Us.* Oxford University Press, New York, N.Y. 230 pp.

• Carson, Rachel. 1962. *Silent Spring.* Houghton Mifflin Co., Boston, Mass. 368 pp.

• Emerson, W.K. and M.K. Jacobson. 1976. *The American Museum of Natural History Guide to Shells: Land, Freshwater and Marine, from Nova Scotia to Florida.* Alfred A. Knopf Inc., New York, N.Y. 482 pp.

• Morris, Percy A. 1973. *A Field Guide to Shells of the Atlantic and Gulf Coasts and the West Indies.* Houghton Mifflin Co., Boston, Mass. 330 pp.

• Rehder, Harald A. 1981. *The Audubon Society Field Guide to North American Seashells.* Alfred A. Knopf Inc., New York, N.Y. 894 pp.

• Solem, G. Alan. 1974. *The Shell Makers. Introducing Mollusks.* John Wiley & Sons, New York, N.Y., 289 pp.

• Turgeon, D.D., A E. Bogan, E.V. Coan, W.K. Emerson, W.G. Lyons, W.L. Pratt, C.F.E. Roper, A. Scheltema, F.G. Thompson and J.D. Williams. 1988. *Common and Scientific Names of Aquatic Invertebrates from the United States and Canada: Mollusks.* Am. Fish. Soc. Spec. Publ. 16. 277 pp.

• Vokes, H.E. and E.H. Vokes. 1983. *Distribution of Shallow-Water Marine Mollusca, Yucatan Peninsula, Mexico.* Mesoamerican Ecol. Inst., Monograph 1, Middle Am. Res. Inst., Tulane Univ., New Orleans, La. Publ. 54. 183 pp.

• Waller, T.R. 1969. *The Evolution of the* Argopecten gibbus *Stock* (Mollusca Bivalvia*) with Emphasis on the Tertiary and Quarternary Species of Eastern North America.* J. Paleontology 43(5):125 pp. Supplement.

• Warmke, G.L. and R.T. Abbott. 1961. *Caribbean Seashells: A Guide to the Marine Mollusks of Puerto Rico and Other West Indian Islands, Bermuda and the Lower Florida Keys.* Livingston Publ. Co., Narberth, Pa. 346 pp.

• Yonge, C.M. and T.E. Thompson. 1926. *Living Marine Mollusca. Collins*, St. James Place, London. 288 pp.